OXFORD MONOGRAPHS ON SOCIAL ANTHROPOLOGY

General Editors

E. E. EVANS-PRITCHARD   B. E. B. FAGG

D. F. POCOCK   A. MAYER

THE MURLE

RED CHIEFS
AND
BLACK COMMONERS

B. A. LEWIS

OXFORD
AT THE CLARENDON PRESS
1972

Oxford University Press, Ely House, London W. 1

GLASGOW NEW YORK TORONTO MELBOURNE WELLINGTON
CAPE TOWN IBADAN NAIROBI DAR ES SALAAM LUSAKA ADDIS ABABA
DELHI BOMBAY CALCUTTA MADRAS KARACHI LAHORE DACCA
KUALA LUMPUR SINGAPORE HONG KONG TOKYO

67103

PRINTED IN GREAT BRITAIN
AT THE UNIVERSITY PRESS, OXFORD
BY VIVIAN RIDLER
PRINTER TO THE UNIVERSITY

TO
THE MURLE
FOR WHOM THIS WAS
WRITTEN

FOREWORD

VERY little has been written about the Murle, called Beir in early literature. The late Mr. Lewis's book therefore fills a big gap in the ethnography of the Southern Sudan.

Mr. Lewis, a graduate of Cambridge (Jesus College), joined the Sudan Political Service in 1930 and served in it for more than twenty years—in Dongola, Khartoum, Upper Nile, Blue Nile, Darfur, and Equatoria. In the course of this service he took a great interest in the customs and institutions of the native peoples, especially the peoples of Darfur and the Nuer and Murle of the Upper Nile. With the encouragement of the Government of the Anglo-Egyptian Sudan he spent four leaves, between 1947 and 1950, at the Institute of Social Anthropology at Oxford (Exeter College) where he received the degree of B.Sc. for a thesis on the Murle which forms the basis of this book. He died rather suddenly while revising the book for publication and the revision was completed by his widow.

It is very unlikely that the research my friend Bazett Lewis did among the Murle can ever be repeated, so we must be grateful to him and to Mrs. Lewis that it is to appear in print.

E. E. E-P.

PREFACE

MY husband did not finish this account, on which he spent much time and endeavour, before his death. I have, therefore, tried to finish shaping it into the form he intended. There are gaps and omissions which I cannot fill. Some years have now elapsed since the material for the book was assembled, and some of the Murle mentioned by name may no longer hold the positions ascribed to them.

An exact translation of certain words is difficult, e.g. *korok*, the fundamental unit of social and economic life. I have therefore retained the author's interpretation of it as 'homestead'. Similarly with *ri*, 'club', the meeting-place of the village elders: I have used this translation rather than 'the meeting-tree', as used by other writers.

There is a considerable number of manuscript notes, and related diagrams and symbols, elicited from the old men and recorded in Murle by Ngacingol, Araani, and Baabanen. These are deposited at the Institute of Social Anthropology, Oxford.

Although many people have given invaluable assistance and advice, few of them are known to me by name. For this reason I make no acknowledgements, though gratitude is implicit.

R. L.

Charlton Mackrell

CONTENTS

Contents   xiii

I

INTRODUCTION

THE Murle are a small tribe of some 18,000 to 20,000 people inhabiting about 10,700 square miles of territory in the Pibor District of the Southern Sudan. Most of their lands lie in the Lotilla valley, although the Hills Murle live on the Maruwa hills to the south-east, and the Boma plateau. This is really a crop of outliers from the Ethiopian mountains rising to 4,000 feet above sea level, whereas the Lotilla valley is part of the huge Upper Nile plain, which is flooded during the rains and almost waterless in summer, at a level of only 1,500 feet above sea level. Pibor District belongs to the Upper Nile Province, and in the south-east the tribal boundary coincides with the Province and international frontier with Ethiopia.

In this account I have four aims: to write a brief historical account of the Murle under the Condominium Government from 1898 to 1955; to record what they told me of their society before their conquest by that Government in 1912; to observe the workings of their society in the early nineteen-forties, when I was their District Commissioner (December 1941–June 1944); and finally to assess the changes which their society underwent during that period.

Each has its own difficulties. The historical records are scanty, Murle memories are long, but as they are a pre-literate society, their history is embedded in a mass of old songs and folklore which was not easy to unravel. My own time with them was far too short, only two and a half years; and finally, as if the assessment of the changes taking place was not sufficiently complex, it was doubly so for me, because for a time, as their District Commissioner, I myself played an active part in this process.

No one is more aware of the shortcomings and omissions in this account than myself. I have done my best to undertake a task for which, probably, no one else is qualified. In doing so I hope to make a slight contribution to the history of a little-known corner of Africa, and to the social anthropology of East Africa, for with the coming of the Independent Sudanese Government in 1955 a chapter was closed in this area, for good or ill, and a new one begun. With the latter I am not concerned, only with trying to make the best possible record of the former, in the hope that it may one day be of interest to the descendants of the Murle I knew.

1. *Early Travellers*

Amongst the early travellers to the Upper Nile region I could find practically nothing about the Murle, except in John Petherick's book *Travels in Central Africa*, published in 1869. He refers to them by their Anuak name 'Ajibba', and although there is no direct evidence in his writings that he ever visited their country, his comments are so accurate that it seems probable that he did so. He writes:

... the Djibba negroes to the South. The latter, apparently with a mixture of Galla in them speak a different dialect and vary in colour from the jet black of the Dinka and Shillok to a dark copper colour. Their manners and customs also differ. Although they do not scalp their fallen enemies, they cut off the hair of their heads and interweave it with their own to form ear lapels, or sometimes a long tail reaching to the ankles. This they ornament with a thick coating of cowrie shells, and add a few ostrich feathers to its extremity. Unlike the former they are not absolutely naked, but wear a hide suspended from the shoulder, falling around the loins; and their faces show a stronger growth of beard, which the black negro, except in rare instances, is almost without.

My having been possessed of some of the weapons and ornaments of the Djibba, the annexed sketch, which illustrates an article I had the honour to read in 1860 at the United Service Institution, and was printed in their journal, will give a better idea of a native of this tribe than any description I can convey. The ornament on the arm is of massive ivory, and the sharp-edged missile in his right hand is of hard wood, and to preserve it from being blunted it is covered with a leather case.[1]

It is said that there was a trading-post at Akobo during the days of the Egyptian Government, so that he may have visited it and there met a few Murle and acquired specimens of some of their weapons and ornaments; but it seems more likely that he actually visited their country. The Murle do not recall any slave raids from

[1] The design on the cover of Petherick's book is supposed to represent a Murle, and is reproduced as an illustration on p. 6 of *Travels in Central Africa*, vol. ii.

the north, although they remember one from Bor and several from the highlands of Abyssinia. In any case, the Pibor river is so narrow and tortuous and so thickly fringed with weeds that it would have been very difficult for Sudanese sailing-boats to navigate. Owing to their inaccessibility, it can probably be safely assumed that they were in fact little troubled by the unwelcome attentions of slave-traders from the Northern Sudan.

Petherick's observations appear to be accurate; although no age-set is now remembered as having worn a long 'tail of human hair', it is quite possible that one of them did so in the past, as the typical Murle headdress is often made with borrowed hair. Many of them are copper-coloured although the majority are black-skinned, like the Nuer and Dinka, and some are intermediate. They certainly grow better beards than their Nilotic neighbours the Anuak, Nuer, and Dinka.

In 1888 Count Teleki and von Höhnel[1] met the Ngandarec branch of the Murle on the Omo river, a few miles to the north of its mouth in Lake Rudolf, and in 1895 Donaldson Smith also came across them. However, this little group was not sufficiently important to secure more than the briefest mention, as its home is only a large village. Bottego, the Italian explorer who traversed Anuak country, also met the Murle at Ukwaa on the Upper Akobo in 1897, while parties of Marchand's French mission to Fashoda led by de Bonchamps (1897) and Faivre (1898) also traversed a corner of their country.

In 1899 Captain M. S. Wellby passed along the Anuak–Murle boundary, but it is not very clear from his book[2] exactly where he went. After the reconquest of the Sudan surveying parties under H. H. Austin (1900)[3] and C. W. Gwynn (1902) were sent by the Sudan Government to map and demarcate the frontiers with Ethiopia, but there is practically nothing in their accounts which throws any light on the Murle of those days.

In 1904 Sir Northrup MacMillan led an expedition of two launches up the Sobat river. Two members of this expedition, C. W. L. Bulpett and B. M. Jessen, trekked from the Sobat across Anuak, using mules and donkeys, and reached the Boma plateau

---

[1] L. V. von Höhnel, 'The Lake Rudolf Region', *Journal of the Royal African Society* (January 1938).

[2] M. S. Wellby, 'Twixt Sirdar and Menelik'.

[3] H. H. Austin, *Among Swamps and Giants in Equatorial Africa*, C. Arthur Pearson Ltd., London, 1902.

in June. They succeeded in getting 'on to very friendly relations and they willingly bartered their ripe corn for beads'.[1] They spent a few days there before trekking back to the Akobo where they were on friendly terms with Chief Ulimi at Ukwaa. They found Boma peaceful, isolated, and prosperous, with large fields of ripening millet. Jessen, who included a short list of Murle words in his book, wrote:

The people living in this mountain fastness were strong, tall and handsome, and seemed to be a much superior race to the Yamboes (Anuak). They were fearless and most decided in their manners though suspicious of any kind of hostility. . . . They must be good hunters as they had skins of giraffe, zebra and various kinds of antelopes. They seemed to have no domestic animals, except goats, and lived chiefly on agriculture. Better durra or cornfields I have never seen anywhere, and they seemed to cultivate every available spot. Villages and cultivated fields were hidden away in the most romantic spots. . . . Some of them came to the camp with all their war finery and looking like demons, but never at any time did they prove unfriendly.[2]

In August and September 1904 Captain Comyn led an expedition to explore the Agwei and Pibor rivers and, more by accident than design, made the first official contact with the Murle. The rivers were in high flood that year and he succeeded in getting far up the River Kengen, a feat which has never since been equalled. His visit is well remembered by the Murle, and referred to as the year of the funnel, *irkit ci oderrima*, in memory of his gunboat. This is the first date I was able to establish for certain in their history.

Fortunately, in addition to his official report published in *Monthly Intelligence Reports*, he wrote a full account of his journey in his book *Service and Sport in the Sudan*: 'Arrived at Nasser I organised my force which consisted of: the gunboat Abu Klea and barge for carrying wood, a small screw launch; a steel Hyslop sailing boat.'[3] There follows a long account of sudd-cutting and other navigational difficulties. When he did succeed in making

[1] C. W. L. Bulpett, *A Picnic Party in Wildest Africa*, Edward Arnold, London, 1907.
[2] B. H. Jessen, *W. N. MacMillan's Expeditions and Big Game Hunting in Southern Sudan, Abyssinia and East Africa*, Marchant Singer & Co., London, 1906.
[3] D. C. E. A. Comyn, *Service and Sport in the Sudan*, John Lane, The Bodley Head, London, 1911.

contact with the Murle the difficulties of translation arose: '. . . our conversation then proceeded in the following manner. I talked to my Arab servant in broken Arabic; he repeated the sense more or less to the Anuak who translated it into Ajibba. The proceeding, with its corrections was more cumbersome than it sounds.'[1] After travelling some 55 miles up the Pibor river he reached Nyanabok:

When I first appeared with the steam launch at Nyanabok, which is behind some high trees, the inhabitants fled. I went up to one of the villages (groups of 3–10 huts) and put some beads in front of each hut. The following day I returned to the village in the steam launch, which the natives had already seen. I sent the interpreter and one man as an escort to tell the Sheikh I would see him. They came running back, having met with a host of natives with levelled spears. I then went myself, approached a group and gave each man of it some beads—and finding one of them was the Sheikh, possessed myself of his hand, he first waved it off, but when I got it he was trembling all over. After a little talk, in which it appeared that the elder men wished to give me a hearing, but the young ones began to get out of hand, the Sheikh requested me to go back to the launch. I did so—waited some minutes —during which the gunboat arrived with good effect, and returned finding the elder men waiting. The natives were rather truculent, and after three and a half hour's talk they almost ordered me to go to the opposite side of the river and wait there. Seeing that treachery was in the wind, I asked them if ever they had seen firearms. Receiving an answer to the negative, I warned them not to be frightened, and fired my gun. In an instant the long grass was alive with flying forms, quite 700. I therefore gathered the head men, fired a round from every gun and revolver with me into a tree, and a saluting cartridge from the gun, and explained, though explanation was not necessary, that I came on a friendly mission, but would stand no nonsense. They then assured me that their country was ours and our friends theirs, and I proceeded to cut wood. The following day we again had a long talk; they wishing to know why we came there at all, seeing that no one had done so before. Did we want to raid for slaves etc.? Some of them sold a little corn in the ear and ivory rings and bracelets for handkerchiefs and beads. The Sheikh brought me a present of a fat-tailed sheep. All through the Agibba country the attitude was friendly (through fear) but suspicious. They refused to go on the boat or to help carry wood for hire. At night, on two occasions, the boat moored in mid-stream, had a mass of men on either bank seemingly kept quiet by the elders of the tribe. They shook spears but did nothing hostile. When I called at Nyanabok on my

[1] Ibid.

return I found the place deserted (still suspicious) the natives evidently
thought we would try to raid slaves there before making off. I left some
beads on the path and continued my journey.

The Agibbas are a warlike tribe, feared by and fearing the Nuers. The
other neighbours, Anuaks and Dinkas, they look on with contempt, and
buy their beads from them. The Abyssinians do not harry this part of the
tribe. A few men know the Nuer and Dinka and Anuak dialects. Their
physique is good but their stature not uniform. Many seem to suffer
from slight enlargement of the testicles, and I saw one man with
elephantiasis of the leg. They are armed with spears of various shapes,
a few wrist knives and an oblong shield of giraffe hide, and invariably
carry their head rests to sit on. Their huts are rude, of a bee-hive shape,
and about the same size as the ordinary *tukl*. They appear to have no
canoes, and I saw no fishing spears, though plenty of fish baskets. Their
ivory ornaments are old and small. The principal men wear over the
right elbow a bunch of giraffe tails, the band ornamented with cowrie
shells. Their clothing consists of a belt round the waist (if a man is well
off), a skin behind, often embroidered and edged with beads; most
wear a $3\frac{1}{2}$ inch band of red beads with a one inch line down the centre
across their foreheads. Some of the older men had a bead-covered bowl
on their heads instead. The hair of the younger men was dressed very
neatly, like an inverted soup-plate with the part over the forehead cut
off. They have all sorts of *suk-suk*. What they asked for were (in order
of preference) cowrie shells, beads, ginators, brass wire, red, white,
and other beads. The head Sheikh, whose name I think is Nadgware
(they were very adverse to telling it), seems a man of character. All
seemed afraid of him, and said that if they took spears without his permission he would cut their throats. I saw but half a dozen women and
no children.[1]

From these extracts it is clear that this first visit must be regarded
as a success; contact was made and hostilities avoided. With the
benefit of hindsight it seems a tragedy that this encounter was not
followed up by the Province authorities. As it turned out, the next
moves came from Bor, where the Government was anxious to
protect the Dinka of the District. In August 1905 H. D. E. O'Sul-
livan, acting Governor of the Upper Nile Province, reported that
the latest Beir (Murle) raids on the Dinka were on Biong in December 1903, on Abang in December 1904, and on Fiul in July 1905.
He added that the 'Dinka were in no such panic as the Mamur's
report might suggest', and that the Beir only raided the outer line

---

[1] *Monthly Intelligence Reports*, 1904 and 1905.

of Dinka villages to the east, about one day's march from Bor, and
that they had never come inside this line—for, fear, apparently that
the Dinkas might combine and cut them off. He continued:

The reason their raids are still possible is because the Dinka will not
combine to repel or punish them; if one village is raided the whole idea
of the others is to keep clear.

He recommended:

It is impossible to ensure the safety of the outer line of Dinka villages
except by a strong patrol into the Beir country, which by inflicting
a heavy fine of cattle or durra may make them think twice before again
raiding tribes under Government protection.[1]

There followed a patrol, the Beir Reconnaissance of 1905, to the
villages on the Upper Kengen, but it failed in its object of preventing the Murle raids on the Dinka, for Miralai R. C. R. Owen,
Governor of Mongalla Province, wrote in his instructions to the
Officer Commanding Beir Patrol in 1908:

The object of this patrol is to punish the Beir tribe for their annual
raids on the Bor Dinka. His Excellency the Governor General is particularly anxious there should be no bloodshed if possible, but I am con-
fident that you will find it impossible to bring them to terms without
strong measures.

If you find it possible you must inform them that the Government
demand a fine in cattle, the restoration of all cattle and prisoners (if any
left alive) also the head chief and several of his prominent men must
return with you to Bor to see me. Another condition of their submission
must be that a certain number of their prominent men must stay at
Mongalla for the good behaviour of the tribe.[2]

The first Beir Patrol started from Bor on 2 June under the
command of Kaimakam J. Wood Martin, Officer Commanding
11th Sudanese. The Patrol was accompanied by 240 Dinka carriers
as far as Pengko. At Manyabok some 1,100 cattle, said to belong to
Chief Lom's people, were rounded up, killing two Murle and
having Bimbashi Ryan stabbed in the process. The Patrol then
advanced to Nyangkobal: there were three night alarms on the
nights of 7 and 8 June, and after some scouting forays the Patrol
withdrew to Manyabol on 9 June. Heavy rain hampered its movements, and so the Patrol withdrew with the captured cattle to

---

[1] Ibid.   [2] Sudan Government correspondence.

Pengko. The Officer Commanding Patrol called for 100 volunteers
from the Dinka to act as carriers for a further visit to Murle
country, but all the Dinka refused. On 15 June the troops set out
with mules only and marched eastwards again, but further heavy
rain made the country practically impassable; on 18 June the
decision was taken to withdraw.

Although the Murle had been fined 1,100 head of cattle and lost
two men in the foray, no progress had been made towards bringing
them under administration or winning their confidence. In fact
they had even less reason to trust the Government than before,
so that it is not surprising that they continued to raid the Dinka.
This flouting of authority could not, of course, be allowed to continue, and in 1912 came the second Beir Patrol, a much more
ambitious project than the first had been. It was organized in three
columns; the northern, which advanced southwards up the Pibor
river from Akobo; the central moving eastwards from Bor, and the
southern column, which never reached Murle country, from Mongalla.

The central column, under command of Major Drake, concentrated at Pengko on 4 January and reached a pool on the
Upper Veveno on 9 January, after a most trying march, owing to
the complete lack of water or shade on the way. On 18 January
it advanced to the junction of the Veveno and Lotilla rivers. Here
it was joined by the northern column, which reported that Baati
Chamchor (drumchief of the Tangajon) had himself come in and
asked for Government protection, after a slight skirmish in which
some cattle had been captured, but that he had paid only ten
cattle of the tax of fifty levied on his section of the tribe as a sign
of submission. After waiting until 23 January for the southern
column the other two moved on towards the river Kengen, whither
most of the Beirs had fled. Various marches and counter-marches
followed, until all the Beir chiefs submitted. A fortified post was
built at the junction of the Lotilla and Kengen rivers by Captain
the Hon. R. Bruce, and it was named after him. Soon it was moved
to Nangoltir, a few miles to the north, on higher ground, and
renamed Pibor Post; to quote the official report: 'The result of the
patrol was the capture of many cattle, sheep and goats, the sub-
jugation and exploration of the Beir country. Our losses (central
and northern columns) were 41 killed and wounded including
friendly Dinkas. The enemy's losses were estimated at 146 killed,

the number of wounded being unknown.'[1] On 15 March the troops withdrew to Akobo, and by 26 April all the Beir chiefs had tendered their submission to Captain the Hon. R. Bruce, who was left in charge of the garrison in the Beir country.

2. *Military Administration*

The Murle were now conquered, and until 1925 formed part of the Sobat–Pibor Military District. What the official report does not state is that the senior Tangajon drum was burnt when the hut in which it was stored was fired by the troops, and the Bournian drumchief of the Ngaloaga Ngarotti lost his only son and heir, Munang, who was shot dead while running away with his small son on his shoulders; the latter was carried off by the troops and brought up in Malakal. The Murle say that Burnian, who had never enjoyed good health, was a broken man after this disaster and for the rest of his life took little part in tribal affairs.

The same year Major Darley, the elephant hunter who withdrew down the Akobo river shortly after the end of this campaign, had spent a whole year on the Upper Kengen, living on amicable terms with the Murle, whom, of course, he supplied with ample quantities of elephant meat. The site of his old encampment, known as *korok ci mersungo*, was pointed out to me in 1942, and I met one of his party at Boma. In his book[2] he paints a very different picture of the state of affairs on Boma from that given by Jessen and Bulpitt in 1904. It was then, in 1912, a centre for Abyssinian raiding parties from Maji, and these were to be the main preoccupation of the garrison at Pibor Post for many years to come.

During the period of the military administration a British Officer was always stationed at Pibor Post. With the exception of Bimbashi Hutten, who was there from 1912 to 1915 and learned to speak a little Murle, none of them stayed for more than a year. Colonel Logan, who had commanded the northern column of the second Beir Patrol, was the first Commanding Officer of the Sobat–Pibor Military District, and wrote articles on 'Manners and Customs of the Beirs', which were published first in *Monthly Intelligence Reports* (August 1913), and subsequently in the first volume

[1] *Monthly Intelligence Reports*, 1912.
[2] Henry Darley, *Slaves and Ivory*, Witherby, London, 1926.

of *Sudan Notes and Records* (October 1918), partly from the personal observations of Bimbashia Hutten and Maclaine, who had been patrolling constantly during the dry season of 1912–13, and partly from the Beirs themselves. Captains Wauchope and H. H. Kelly, political officers to the northern and central columns, also wrote reports on them, which were published in *Monthly Intelligence Reports* of 1912. Colonel C. R. K. Bacon, who succeeded Colonel Logan and remained in charge at Akobo until 1925, acquired some influence with the Murle chiefs: he used to make a long trek every dry-weather season, and his contributions to the mapping of the area—an essential preliminary task—were remarkable. His chief preoccupations were always with the international frontier with Ethiopia, and the Anuak on both sides of this frontier, as they were to be with his civilian successors.

3. *Civil Administration, 1925–1954*

In 1924, when the future of the area was under discussion, and prior to its inclusion in the civil administration of the Upper Nile Province, Colonel Bacon begged the Sudan Government to appoint two District Commissioners—one for the Anuak and the other for the Murle—predicting that otherwise progress would be no faster than under the military administration. In the event the Government felt that it could not afford two officials for the Anuak-Beir District, as it was then called, since it produced so little revenue.

As Colonel Bacon had foretold, the District Commissioner had to devote most of his time to the Anuak and their frontier troubles with Ethiopia, so that the Murle, who were then quiet, were left very much to themselves for the next eleven years.

There was a District reorganization in 1935, when the neighbouring Abwong District was split, the Dinka part being transferred to the Central Shilluk District, while Captain Alban, with the Lou Nuer he had for long administered, was transferred to the new Pibor District, with headquarters at Akobo. Mr. John Winder (subsequently Governor, Upper Nile Province) was his assistant.

Captain Alban was an administrator of many years' experience in this part of the world. He had served with Driberg amongst the Didinga at Nagichot some years before, and mistrusted what he called 'Mongalla methods'. He had no easy task in starting to administer the Murle, for the Lou Nuer raided them at Kottome on the Nanaam river in April 1937, killing seventeen Murle and capturing many women, children, and cattle. This naturally took some time to settle, and Mr. Winder, who visited the Murle in October, when he collected much new and valuable information, was transferred at the end of the year. Following this visit Mr. Winder wrote two unpublished articles, 'Notes on the Murle Tribe' and 'Notes on the Age-Set System Amongst the Murle', which were a great advance on anything previously written.

Most of the working season of 1937–8 was spent by Captain Alban in settling the Kottome raid and handing over the Lou Nuer to Captain W. H. B. Lesslie, who had succeeded Mr. Winder at the end of 1937. During the next two years some progress was achieved; chiefs' courts were set up at Lokwangoli on the main river, at Pibor Post, at Gummuruk on the Veveno, and at Ferteit on the Kengen, the chiefs and elders being left to settle any cases that arose. The great difference from the past was that anyone who felt he had a grievance could come to the District Commissioner and have his case referred to the chiefs and elders. Tribute in the form of 170 bulls was assessed and collected; a number of chiefs were recognized as Government chiefs and paid small salaries; chiefs' police were appointed and attached to them.

On 10 June 1940, however, the Italians, then rulers of Ethiopia, declared war, and progressive administration was again halted. Before the end of June, when the rains set in and prevented further movement in the area, Captain Alban had captured the Italian posts at Tirguol and Kwonyeret on the opposite bank of the Pibor river, thus securing his communications by river with Province Headquarters at Malakal.

During the 1940–1 dry season the Murle were left entirely unvisited, because Captain Alban, with various outside assistance, was directing the operations of the Gila Force in Anuak country inside Abyssinia. This local war was brought to a successful conclusion with the capture of Gambeila in 1941, when the Italians were driven out of the Baro salient, but, tragically, Captain Lesslie was killed when this action was almost over.

By then there was little time left for normal administrative work in the District before the 1941 rains. In any case, Captain Alban's health had been undermined and he was sent home on sick leave. I was appointed to succeed him in Pibor District in December 1941, and with him made my first visit to the Murle in January 1942. While we were there, news was received from Bor and Torit that five Lafon traders were missing and presumed killed by the Murle. We raised this matter at Gummuruk but the chiefs denied all knowledge. Kortulia, the Government interpreter, and some of the Tangajon chiefs' police who were with us, were sure that something had happened, but could discover no details. After a few days Captain Alban announced to the chiefs that, as they had not taken any action, he was obliged to do so, and accordingly fined them 170 cattle—20 for each of the missing men, 30 for their merchandise, and 40 for the Government as a fine; and he told the President of the Court, Kengen Baatalan, to see that they were produced at Pibor Post within two months. He was doubtful whether the fine would materialize, and, in case of default, he was most insistent that I should punish the section responsible.

We then returned to Lou Nuer to supervise the chiefs' courts there. This took us until well into March, when Captain Alban went on to the Adonga Anuak, while C. G. Davies, Governor of the Province, and I drove to Pibor Post and on up the Kengen river to Boma. We returned through Kapoeta and Torit, where we picked up a delegation from Lafon, drove on to Juba, and returned to Akobo via Bor. As Captain Alban had anticipated, the fine had not been paid, although his time limit had expired. In the late afternoon a few days later I set off once again for Pibor Post, with three lorries, twenty Government police, and twenty Nuer chiefs' police. We reached Pibor Post after dark, and continued our journey in the early hours of the following morning, arriving at Gummuruk before dawn. We then drove across country and up the bed of the Lotilla to Belmorok, some thirty miles to the south, in the area where the culprits were supposed to be hiding. Here we found three large herds of cattle, rounded them up, and started to drive them off. We were attacked by the Murle, who managed to stampede the herd in front. Bullets began to fly and one policeman was speared. Late that night, however, some 500 cattle were safely *kraaled* at Gummuruk, and the following morning the Murle chiefs came in to protest. Explaining that I was aware I had impounded the wrong cattle, I made them understand that I was prepared to exchange them for those of the real culprits, and as the owners of the captured cattle came to claim their beasts the story began to unravel. It transpired that twelve young men had set on the Lafon traders, seized all their goods, and left them to die of thirst on their way to Bor. I let it be known that I wanted each of these young men with twenty cattle apiece, and soon small parties of my force, led by the cattle owners, were searching for the offenders. As soon as one was produced with his fine I released those belonging to their rightful owners. I tried my utmost to impress on them that I wanted justice rather than the indiscriminate punishment of the innocent, and although the chiefs and owners soon took my point and began to co-operate, it took well over a month to complete the operation.

The Lafon delegation were delighted with their 140 cattle and drove them back via Lou Nuer and Bor. In addition, twenty head of cattle were paid to the head of the family of the man who had been killed during the rounding-up, and I rewarded those I felt had deserved it, still leaving a balance of cattle for the Government fines fund. The prisoners were sent to Malakal, not so much to undergo imprisonment, as to show them something of the Government's power. There, for the first time, they saw aeroplanes, police in number, and steamers on the Nile; but it was the telephone and tap water that appeared to impress them most. after three months' detention they were returned to Akobo and released.

After the rains I was joined by Mr. J. N. Grover, who took over the Anuak. I had learned Nuer while in charge of the Zeraf District in 1935–8, and so was able to start learning Murle as soon as I arrived in Akobo; a slow process I found it, through Nuer and Arabic, trying to write my own grammar and vocabularies as I went along. All through the period of the military administration, and afterwards, the interpreters were very poor, only speaking the most rudimentary Arabic. The night the Murle chiefs decided they could talk to me without the aid of an interpreter they sent my Murle servant Leuwa to wake me, told me to take my notebook and pencil, and preferred no less than sixteen complaints against Kortulia, the official interpreter.

I had arrived in Nuerland at the end of 1935, not long after Nuer settlement; returning in 1942, I was greatly encouraged to note the progress which had been achieved with wild, proud, and untamed people by a handful of District Commissioners who had taken the trouble to learn the language. In trying to deal with the Nuer of the Zeraf I had studied Professor E. E. Evans-Pritchard's writings on them; such anthropology as I knew had been learned in the 'long grass' (as this part of the country is known to those who have served there). When trying to repeat the process with the Murle, I had to find out for myself how their social and political systems worked, and I determined to leave something on record for my successors, particularly as the then Civil Secretary, the late Sir Douglas Newbold, had made me promise to do so. This account, with all its shortcomings, is the result.

After two and a half years as their District Commissioner I was sent home on sick leave, following a particularly severe bout of malaria. During this time I began to think about their political organization and customary law, knowledge of which was essential for their administration. In 1949 I was granted sixty days' special duty to complete my studies in the area, and this was primarily devoted to the kinship system. By then I had spent two leave periods (in 1947 and 1948) studying anthropology at Oxford under Professor Evans-Pritchard.

My return visit to the Murle was far more productive than any comparable period while I was their District Commissioner, for by then I had a good team of Murle assistants and no administrative duties to distract my attention. Ngacingol, Araani, Baabanen, and Kereero, whom I had sent to school at Nasir, could now all write and speak English; and although they were poor informants in themselves, they were invaluable in recording what the old men had to say in Murle, and then helping me to translate the texts. Initially the Murle were very shy and suspicious, but gradually they found I was genuinely interested in their customs, and some of them took pains to ensure that I understood them correctly. In order to get them talking I used to explain Nuer behaviour and then ask what they did in similar circumstances. Almost invariably they found the comparison so interesting that they responded easily, while I listened and observed as much as possible.

By 1949 considerable progress in the administration of the District had been achieved. Mr. R. E. Lyth, who had taken over the Anuak and Murle from Mr. Grover at the end of 1943, was an ex-missionary, recruited into the Sudan Defence Force for the Italian campaign, and stationed on Boma in charge of the military garrison there from 1942 to 1945. He had started to learn Murle at the same time as myself, indeed, we had tried to co-operate, but the difficulties of communication then made it practically impossible. Eventually Mr. Lyth wrote an excellent grammar and dictionary. He also made a new road to Boma, branching off from the Pibor Post–Pochalla road, opened by Mr. Grover through the Maruwa hills. In fact, all the roads had improved. In addition he had taught them to frame-dry their hides, thus securing far higher prices for them at the periodical auctions. Merchants' shops had been laid out in a small tree-lined market just to the north of the police lines in Pibor Post, and he had done his best to stimulate trade and the use of money by the tribe. During Mr. Lyth's tenure of office he had instituted a census, largely the work of Ngacingol, who was then District Clerk, so that it was possible to turn over to a cash tribute on a poll-tax basis, and he had actively supported the medical and educational work of the American Mission on the opposite side of the river at Pibor Post.

It was, in all, a most encouraging improvement from the state of affairs I had originally found in 1942, although inevitably much still remained to be done to catch up on the years of inadequate administration. This second visit led me to make certain recommendations to the central government to bring the Murle into line with the pattern of local government then evolving in the rest of the country. Of these the most important were medical, for although my investigations into the kinship system were far from being a full sociological survey of the Murle family (I had neither the time nor the means at my disposal for this), I had come to the conclusion that there was something radically wrong with the Murle birth-rate, which called for a proper inquiry.

I was, therefore, delighted to hear in 1958 from Kerar effendi Ahmed Kerar, the first Sudanese District Commissioner after Independence, that he had carried out all my recommendations, including a medical campaign against venereal disease. Subsequently, in 1961, Araani, then on a course at the Institute of Education, London University, visited my wife and I in Somerset and gave me the welcome news that following the success of this campaign women were again bearing children, with considerable gain to tribal morale and happiness.

My last visit to the Murle in March 1953 was necessarily very brief—I was then stationed in Juba and could spare only a few days, but had been working during the evenings on the old songs with Ngacingol, while he was on a course of instruction for junior executive officers. Araani was then being trained as a schoolmaster at Mundri, and Baabanen as a veterinary assistant at Malakal.

He eventually became the first Murle member of the Sudanese Parliament. In addition, other Murle boys were following in their footsteps to provide a nucleus of officials for the administration and development of their country.

Previously I had spent four years at Geneina in Western Darfur, on the boundaries of the old kingdoms of Darfur and Wadai, lands of the so-called Tchado-Hamitic peoples. In these kingdoms the remains of the old pre-Arab organization in four districts still persist. Sir Harold MacMichael writes of the Fur District of Kerne, north of the River Azum, subject to the Fur functionary called the Niamaton. The area south of the Azum is the district or *dar* of the Abo Dima, known in Zalingei District as the Dimingawi, an arabicized version of his name:

Now Kerne which is the western division of the old Fur Kingdom means the 'trousers of the Sultan' while Dar Tekanyawi is the great northern division now inhabited by Zaghawa, Tunjur and Arabs.[1]

These four divisions were confirmed to me verbally, and it is clear from Omar el Tunisi's book[2] that similar divisions used also to exist in that kingdom. I found many smaller tribes in the area had copied this organization—split into two halves along the axis and divided into twelve sections in each half, with six sections in each district, and if not in fact so divided, they felt they should be. I drew this pattern for Ngacingol and he said that it summed up the Murle plan.

During my visit in 1953 I drew this pattern in the sand for the benefit of various elders. They laughed and said 'That's it', and pointing to the intersection in the centre asked if I knew what it was called. When I shook my head, they replied 'The place of blessing, *nga ci tovento*'.[3] For me this reduced their complex political, military, and kinship organization to a simple geometrical pattern. I also tried to investigate their religion and thought during these few days, but time was desperately short for such an enthralling and involved subject.

Culturally the Murle clearly fall into what is called the Nilo-Hamitic group of tribes, but this is, strictly speaking, a linguistic

---

[1] Sir Harold MacMichael, *A History of the Arabs in the Sudan*, vol. i, Cambridge University Press, 1922, pp. 97–100.
[2] Mohammed Ibn Omar el Tounsy, *Voyage au Ouaday*, Paris, 1851.
[3] Cf. pp. 32, 60.

term, and the Murle–Didinga language has often been described as belonging to this group. However, Dr. A. N. Tucker, of the School of Oriental Studies, London University, told me that he considered this an over-simplification. He wrote:

There is a very close vocabulary connection between all the languages usually called 'Nilo-Hamitic' (Bari, Lotulla, Topotha, Karamojong, Teso, Masai, etc., and the Nandi–Kipsigis group) which is not echoed in the Murle–Didinga group. In fact there is a closer vocabulary link between them and the Nilotic languages than between either and Murle. Grammatically the distinction is wider and the very behaviour of Murle–Didinga is closer to that of Tama than anything else.

He therefore classified Murle–Didinga as an 'isolated language group', pending further information on the subject.

Miss M. A. Bryan has examined the relationship between the Tama and Didinga language groups in an article published by the Deutsche Akademie der Wissenschaften zu Berlin, Institut für Orientforschung, Veröffentlichung Nr. 26, 1955. She does not reach any very definite conclusions, but does mention certain resemblances between the two groups—Tama, Sungor, Mararit, and Kebit on the one hand (all tribes on the Darfur–Wadai border), and the Murle, Longarim, Didinga group on the Sudan–Ethiopian border on the other. Briefly, she finds little lexical correspondence between the two groups of languages, although in both groups there is a multiplicity of singular and plural suffixes to nouns and some of the morphemes show correspondence: of these, however, some are found in the Nilo-Hamitic languages, in Temein (spoken in the Nuba Hills), and in the Daju language, which has representatives in Wadai, Darfur, and Kordofan. It is the pattern of verbal conjugation in the two groups which shows a remarkable resemblance, and is unlike that found in any other known language in Africa. This Tama group of languages is also classified by Miss Bryan and Dr. Tucker as an 'isolated language group'.[1]

It is obviously difficult to determine the exact implication of this linguistic resemblance between two groups of tribes now so widely separated, but it is significant that there should be a linguistic similarity, however small, besides that on the cultural plane in the four-fold division of the tribes. One can also compare the religious

---

[1] *Handbook of African Languages*, vol. iv: *The Non-Bantu Languages of North-East Africa*, Oxford 1956.

C

significance of pythons, which obtains in Dar Tama, the Fur,[1] and other tribes on the Wadai border, as amongst the Murle.[2]

I paid only the briefest visits to the Didinga and Longarim in the Boya Hills, but these tribes were evidently at one time parts of the same tribe. Almost all that Driberg wrote about the Didinga is applicable to the Murle. The quarrel between the Longarim and the Murle is well remembered[3] and took place not so many generations ago at Medainya, a small watercourse below the Boma plateau. It was caused by a dispute over some soup made from an oribi which was all that had been killed that day. While I was District Commissioner Pibor I wrote to the District authorities at Kapoeta to find out if the Longarim had drums, and the reply was in the negative, but when I visited the Longarim with Colonel P. de Roebeck in 1952 I asked them the same question myself. They replied 'No', so I went on to explain about the drums, and they replied 'O yes! We have *kidong ci tammu* or *kidong ci Murlu*' ('sky drums' or 'Murle drums'), and I soon discovered that they too were organized in four drumships. After taking the precaution of sacrificing a goat, Mrs. Mansfield subsequently saw one of these drums, which was kept carefully wrapped up in a cave, but was lacking a skin.

Although it appears that the Longarim have recently been considerably influenced by Topotha customs, '. . . they have adopted many linguistic and verbal expressions, particularly those relating to the "favourite beast complex", the age-system and the institution of the "best friend", from their Nilo-Hamitic neighbours the Tapotha';[4] and since the Didinga have lost their sacred drums, I believe much of what I have written about the Murle is also applicable to them, and that originally they were all members of the same tribe.

[1] Cf. R. Davies, 'Notes on Totemism in the Homr Tribe', *Sudan Notes and Records*, vol. ii, no. 3 (July 1919).
[2] 'Kisu', 'drum', is used by the Fur for one grade of chiefs.
[3] Cf. p. 59.
[4] Dr. A. Kronenberg, 'The Longarim Favourite Beast', *Kush*, ix (1961), pp. 258–77.

II

MURLELAND AND ITS SEASONS

THE Murle are a pre-literate people with an extremely simple material culture. It is impossible to understand their political structure and processes without reference to the environmental and ecological factors. The rhythm of the seasons has a profound effect on their distribution, and the nature of the countryside in which they live has as much effect on their means of livelihood. Both, therefore, are intimately connected with their sense of values —what they consider desirable or the reverse in particular circumstances; what they consider correct behaviour in the important events of life. Tradition and custom, distilled from tribal experience, to a great extent governs their actions, their adjustment to their surroundings, and their arrangements for dealing with the recurrent tasks of the changing seasons.

Respect for their customs, *ker ci Murlu*,[1] is so great that many of them have the force of law; indeed, there are no separate words for law and custom. Although they are primarily interested in the present, their respect for tradition is so ingrained that some investigation of their past history is necessary to appreciate their present way of life.

It is difficult to piece together their history because it is enshrined in songs employing the language of poetry. The Murle are a musical people and their songs are full of allusions, allegory, and imaginative comparisons. Their past can be unravelled only by discussing these songs with the older people, who can explain the references, the archaic expressions with which they abound, and the names of personalities.

1. *Origins and Migrations*

Tradition claims that the tribe was created at Jen[2], far away to the north-east of their present country, beyond Maji in Ethiopia.

---

[1] Cf. p. 72.   [2] Cf. pp. 41, 48.

There are a number of myths and songs about Jen, of which the following extract is typical:

> O! Jen! It was at Jen that our ancestors came down to earth.
> They captured the black cattle.
> Crumble the tobacco for at Jen the tobacco was sweet like cattle.
> Curse the enemy we have met with here.
> They will not let our calves escape from their desert.

These words mean little to them today, but are remembered because Jen is important, symbolizing the East, the source of life, where the tribe began and from whence the rains come. Jen is thus contrasted with *Nyagi*, the West, which is the path of the spirits. To this day corpses are exposed to the west of the homestead and people are supposed to sleep facing the east. It is said that a child which has rolled over in its sleep would be turned to face the east again by its parents.

There are two myths of the creation: the following, which specifically links the creation of the tribe with Jen, is the clearest, and was told me by an old man:

> Long ago at the beginning of time some women came down from heaven to earth at Jen. No men came with them. The next day they went into the bush to cut grass with which to build houses. One of them stooped down to cut a clump of grass and a voice cried out 'Do not cut me!' She looked to see what had spoken and found a spirit in the grass. She caught it, tied it up with grass, and took it home with her. That night the spirit made love to her. Every day she went out to work, leaving the spirit in her hut, and each night the spirit slept with her. In due course she became with child, and the other girls asked who had given her the child. She replied 'God'. One day, when she had gone out to work, two of the other girls went to her hut; they found the spirit and took it away. When she returned that evening there was no trace of the spirit. She asked her companions who had stolen her 'rib', as she called the spirit, and one of them confessed and returned it to its original finder. In due course her child wanted to be born, and the others cut open her stomach and took out the child, but neither survived. Some time later the girl who had stolen the spirit reached her time, and the other girls wanted to cut her open as well, but Rat appeared on the scene and told them to shake her and on no account to cut her open. They did as Rat commanded, and so a boy was born—named Murimaan—who grew up and became the father of all the Murle.

This was how Rat, *Mudec*, helped all mankind. The boy who was helped by Rat, a single man, fathered all the people, and that was how

he was born. The people wanted to reward Rat with a cow, but he said
'No. I am small, I don't want a cow, I want to live in your house and eat
meat and grain and fat.' And that is why to this day all the rats come
when a Kelenya chief dies, and more still when a Kelenya chief's senior
wife dies.[1]

This story is recalled by the following Rabelaisian song, which is
still sung:

> Rip! Rip! You have torn it.
> How shall I find a cow for my mother?
> If my mother had been present then,
> I would have cut off your member with an axe.
> Oh! Girl, don't say that.
> Our thing is good from the beginning of time.

When discussing this story, which seems to suggest that the
creation occurred as a result of seduction without the preliminary
payment of bridewealth, the Murle always say that God created
the people in the sky. Some of them came down to earth and Abei,
the grandmother of all mankind, bore Murimaan, who became the
ancestor of the chiefs. Sometimes they say that Jok begot Murimaan, sometimes that Tammu created the people in heaven. The
word *Tammu* means God, but it also means the rain or the sky.
Jok, on the other hand, means 'the great spirit', and may be a
Nilotic loan word. They say that 'Jok is male, Jok is living in
heaven', and the word used for 'in heaven' is *tamma*, the locative
form of *Tammu*, and in some way which they do not explain precisely, Tammu includes Jok. They say 'they are the same', but
Tammu is more frequently used. I gained the impression that their
philosophy attempted to explain the mystery of the creation by
analogy with a human birth: thus the first birth on earth resulted
from the union of the maleness of the spirit Jok with the flesh of
the woman created by Tammu in heaven, and produced Murimaan.

There are other stories connected with Manidherbo and the
Pleiades,[2] and the Etiwur[3] stories about the finding of different
animals connected with the creation, but these are less clearly
remembered and involve such puzzling contradictions that they
appear to be of far less importance.

[1] Cf. p. 50.
[2] See Chapter VII, pp. 131, 132, and 151.
[3] Cf. Ngenvac Drumship genealogy facing p. 59.

From Jen the Murle say they gradually moved down the River
Omo to Lake Rudolf. There is still a Murle village mentioned by
various travellers on the Omo,[1] which is where the Lotilla Murle
say the Ngandarec lived. Their migration took them on to Kolo-
baadh, in what is now Tapotha country, on to Mount Kathiangor,
which they call Kather, and thence northwards into the Maruwa
hills, one section moving to Boma. It was then that the split
occurred with the Longarim who now inhabit the Boya hills.
Now organized in four drumships of their own, the Longarim
were probably then the junior drumship in the Ngarotti section of
the tribe, as many clans which are regarded as Longarim clans
by the Murle exist to this day in Lotilla, and are all claimed by the
Ngarotti. How far these wanderings were due to pressure from the
'Kum' group of tribes, by which they mean the Tapotha, Jiye, and
Turkana, it is impossible to say. For generations they have been
fighting the Kum,[2] and at present the drying-up of the country
round Lake Rudolf drives the Turkana to encroach on Tapotha
grazing; this process, which has certainly been going on for a
long time, may well be the real cause of the Murle advance from
Mount Kathiangor to Maruwa, and so on to the valley of the
Lotilla which they inhabit today. The last great battles on the
Nyangkobal, as they call the River Veveno, with the former Dinka
inhabitants, who were driven out, are well remembered and
occurred only three or four generations ago. While the Ngarotti
were fighting the less formidable Dinka, the Kelenya were en-
countering much stiffer opposition from the Anuak to the north
and east of their present country, while more recently still the
Tangajon have suffered at the hands of the Nuer, both Lou and
Jekany, who were comparatively late-comers to the area immediately to the north of Murleland. The Murle claim that their
conquest of the Lotilla valley took several years, and probably
occurred four or five generations ago.

This, then, is the world known to the Murle. Their neighbours
are the Nuer and Dinka, both referred to as Jongkodh, who live
to the north and west of them; to the east are the Anuak, known
as Nyuro, who also have a small community on Lafon Hill far to
the south-west, called the 'giraffe's calf Anuak'. Occasional contacts are still made with their cousins the Longarim, who live in

---

[1] Dr. A. Donaldson Smith, *J.R.G.S.* 16 (1900); L. V. von Höhnel, *J.R.A.S.*
xxxvii, No. CXLVI, Jan. 1938.   [2] Cf. p. 89.

the Boya hills north of the Nyaddinga in the Didinga mountains. Due south they are in contact with the Jiye and Tapotha on the upper reaches of the Kengen river. The small Murle community living on the Boma plateau, in the extreme south-east corner of Murleland, are in close contact with the Suri, known as Dhuak, and other small tribes of the Tirma group. East of Boma they also know of the Galla, whom they call Ecumpa, who in the past occasionally raided them from the highlands of Ethiopia.

2. *Hydrology*

The best account of the complicated hydrology of the Lotilla valley is given by Hurst and Phillips.[1] The whole area is a vast, very flat, plain through which flow a series of shallow watercourses. The Veveno and Lotilla derive their water from the run-off of the Imatong and Didinga mountains to the south. Spates rush down the watercourses from these hills during the rains, only to lose themselves in the featureless plains to the north, which become swamps for part of the year. The surface rain water, probably augmented by this run-off, creeps northwards through the grass and eventually collects to form the Veveno, Nanaam, and Lotilla rivers, which drain into the Pibor and so to the Sobat and the Nile. Further east the Akobo and Kongkong rivers and their tributaries drain from the outlying mountains of the Ethiopian escarpment north of Boma, while the River Kengen comes past Mount Kathiangor from the Tirma highlands to the south-east of Boma.

It is only along the rivers that there is any real vegetation. Thin strips of forest or bush line the banks of the watercourses where there is a little slope, and there are often groups of fine trees, but elsewhere the wide plains of black cracking clays stretch for miles, covered by tall grass after the rains. These rivers and their tributaries flow for only a short period, and during most of the year they dry out into a series of pools, although their beds make a ribbon of green through the parched brown countryside. The grey-green leaves and twisted black trunks of the *yoey* tree[2] that fringe the Veveno, Lotilla, and Kengen rivers for many miles give Murleland a distinctive character which is not met with in other parts of the Sudan.

In normal years the rivers do not start to rise until June, although

---

[1] Hurst and Phillips, *The Nile Basin*, vol. ii, Cairo, 1931, p. 99.
[2] *Terminalia spinosa.*

the water of the Akobo and Gila rivers may flood backwards up the lower reaches of the Lotilla in May. During July and August they rise very quickly, reaching their peak in September or early October. They fall even more rapidly than they rise, during October and November, so that by December the main river has normally ceased to flow. In exceptional years—such as saw the floods of 1904, 1917, 1932, and 1946—the whole country is under water at the height of the flood, except for a few eminences, and great hardship is caused to the tribe, their cattle, and the game with which much of their country abounds. The 1932 floods rose 4½ metres above the average flood level. When the extreme flatness of that part of the Upper Nile plain is remembered, the extent of this flooding can be appreciated. The average rise of the rivers is some 2 metres, while in a few dry years it is less than 1.

3. *The Rhythm of the Seasons*

The Murle have no word for the whole year, but speak of two seasons, the wet and the dry, each consisting of six months, and each divided into two parts. The wet season begins with the light rains (*lolongum*), roughly from mid April to mid June, which lead on to the main rains (*loala*)—from about mid June to mid October, when the rivers are full. Similarly the dry season consists of the windy time (*lomoat*), mid October until mid December, followed by the real hot dry season (*tagith*)—mid December to mid April.

The following table shows the average rainfall recorded at Akobo,

AVERAGE RAINFALL (in millimetres)

Month	Akobo	Pibor Post	Boma
January	0·9	6·0	6·5
February	1·7	9·5	15·8
March	19·4	35·9	85·7
April	73·4	84·4	123·6
May	130·7	128·8	210·5
June	119·7	115·7	154·8
July	145·8	134·0	142·0
August	189·6	143·5	329·2
September	140·8	168·6	96·6
October	71·1	70·5	94·8
November	18·2	40·6	54·0
December	2·7	15·7	48·8
Yearly total	914·0	953·2	1,262·3

N.B. These figures do not tally with those in *Agriculture in the Sudan*, ed. J. D. Tothill, Oxford University Press (London), 1948.
For Akobo, see ibid., Table 10, p. 82.

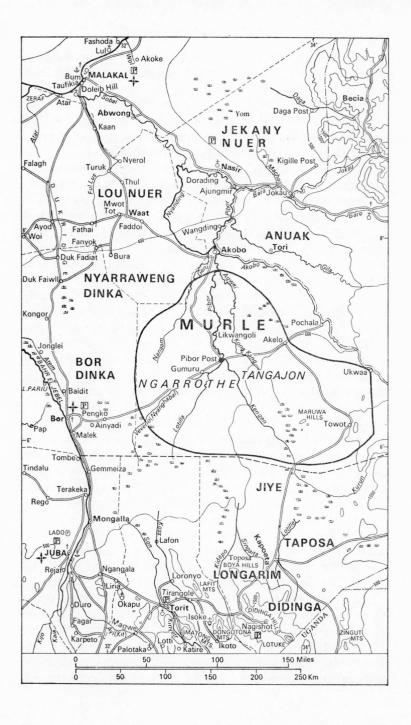

Pibor Post, and Boma. Although a little rain falls in almost every month of the year, the contrast between the two seasons is more marked than this table suggests, because the strong winds of *lomoat*, followed by the hot sun of *tagith*, dry up the countryside until it is parched and brown, while the cloudy days of the wet season produce enough moisture to keep the land cool and green.

Although the Murle say that each season consists of six months, they cannot give names to all the months of the year. Most of them have names, but these refer rather to the activities that take place in each than to an orderly succession of months. The beginning of the windy season is marked by *wagaagac*, when the wind which has been blowing from the south veers round and starts to blow from the north, and often, as they put it, 'does not know which way to blow'. Then comes *dadhau*, the month of the second grain harvest, when the *mowi* ceremonies are held, before the warriors take the cattle out to the camps in search of grazing. *Donycaala*, the month of the game migration from the south, follows, when the north wind often brings cooler weather. Little interest is taken in the long, hot, weary months of *tagith keng*, the 'belly of the dry weather' when the 'world is hot and ugly'. It is not until *ngotobe*, when the first storms occur between intervals of intense heat, that the women start preparing their fields for the new season's crops, mending houses and repairing their fish baskets for the fishing parties that are held in the large remaining pools. These activities are intensified during the following month *ngararon*, more rain falls, and everybody looks for the sowing-star *dumec* to appear over the horizon. Once this is seen happiness abounds, fresh green grass springs up, and consequently milk yields increase; families desert their temporary dry-weather homesteads and work busily in the fields in the cool of the morning, for now the rains have come in earnest. Communications then become difficult; with all the low-lying land either sodden or swampy, the rivers are so swollen that they are often impassable, and so, for the time being, the country is safe from the aggression of hostile neighbours. Then, at last, the warriors come home from their camps, driven to seek the protection of the byres from the clouds of mosquitoes that plague them and their cattle at night when they sleep outside. Homesteads are temporarily reunited; the warriors wear their huge ceremonial head-dresses of human hair, marriages are celebrated, and the main dances held. Once the first crop has been harvested, food is plentiful, milk abundant, and everyone is contented and at peace. All too soon the grazing near the permanent villages is used up, and as the countryside dries out the warriors grow restive under the restraint of the elders, and think about driving the cattle off to fresh pasture and the freedom of their camps, and so the cycle continues.

It is in this rhythm of the seasons rather than the sequence of months that the Murle are interested. Owing to the vagaries of the weather they often make mistakes in the name of the month: if heavy storms break in March they are inclined to rejoice that *ngararon* has come, only to be disillusioned when these are followed by a return to hot dry weather. The importance of time to them is in its occupational value. All are cheerful and eager to perform their appointed tasks after *dumec*, when the bleak brown world of summer has been renewed and clothed in fresh green foliage, while the long wearisome days of the hot weather are endured with stoicism.

4. Concepts of Time

Similarly it is possible to make a fairly complete time-chart for the twenty-four hours of the day from the position of the sun and the daily tasks performed at particular times. As with the seasons, it is the relative value of time that is significant; it is less important in the middle of the night, when everybody should be asleep, or at midday, when most people are resting, than it is in the early morning or the evening. They speak of 'first light', 'dawn', and the 'loosing of the cattle'. Then the sun is 'sweet', and as the day wears on it is first 'ugly', then 'hot', and finally becomes 'deep'. The term *waadh* is used to express day as opposed to night, and is also applied to the long midday period. After *waadh* the sun 'starts to lean'; the cattle return to the homestead, and are driven out again in *yoman*, the late afternoon. Sunset is followed by dusk, when the cattle return to be milked, and after this the evening meal is eaten; then it is night and people go to sleep. Midnight is 'the belly of the night', and about two hours later they say the 'elephant has turned its calf over' (I was unable to discover the reason for this phrase), and the last part of the night is referred to as the 'time of deep sleep'.

Reference is constantly made to the next rains or the last dry season, each one being remembered by reference to some particular event after which it is named. In this way it is possible to make a list for the last thirty or forty years, but beyond that it is difficult to place the years consecutively, because those days have ceased to interest them. The year Captain Comyns visited the Murle in the gunboat *Abu Klea*, 1904, is the first year which can be definitely dated. Almost every year in the past had some notable battle to distinguish it, so that, by reference to the age-sets concerned, the Murle know roughly when it occurred. For practical purposes today this is of little importance, as everything which happened beyond living memory is regarded as having occurred a 'long time ago'. Important events, precedents in cases, or rulings by the chiefs, are remembered in songs; they are not dated, because no need is felt for this. Historical time tends to go back much further from the present day in matters which concern the whole tribe than it does in connection with affairs affecting only a small group within the tribe. Beyond living memory events are remembered only if they affect the structure of the group, as marriages affect the relationship between lineages, or major battles affected the age-sets. In this way it is possible to reckon time in the more distant past by generations or age-sets, but not by seasons.

The days of the month are reckoned by the moon, and the month is divided into two parts: the 'moon' when it is waxing and the 'shade' when it is on the wane. There are special names: for the first day, 'deep sleep'; on the second day 'the cattle see it'; and when the thin sickle of the new moon appears in the sky on the third day, *wiliwili*. Subsequently the days are counted as the fourth or fifth day of the moon, until full moon, *badgol*, because 'it has returned to its place'; the following day is *kiyari*, because it shines with the silvery lustre associated with the mother-of-pearl-like gleam of mussel shells found in the rivers. The following night is known as *tukaltang*, because torches are again needed at milking time.

Differences of opinion do occur over a particular day, but generally, by counting so many days before or after the full or new moon, people manage to assemble on the same day for particular purposes without any difficulty.

5. *Topography and Concepts of Space*

The Murle have the most detailed and accurate knowledge of their own country. Every pool and stream, almost every group of trees and thicket, is known and named, and they can explain to each other by reference to these natural features where a particular camp may be, or where some event took place. Their conception of space, however, is as relative as their notions of time. 'Near' may mean over fifty miles in the dry weather, when a young warrior armed only with a spear is concerned, but would naturally be very far away for an elderly women with a heavy load, ploughing through the mud in the rains.

There are names for the different districts into which their country is divided. Lilota, the 'main' or 'lower' river, is the name of the northern part of the main Pibor river, and is contrasted with the country of the upper rivers, *lel te den*: this is divided into the Veveno, Lotilla, and Kengen, after the rivers which flow through them. Smaller areas are referred to by village names or the name of a stream or pool. Particular types of soil are distinguished by name, while their knowledge of the trees, bushes, plants, and grasses which grow throughout their country is extremely detailed. Children learn to read the signs of the game trails almost as soon as they are able to walk, because game means meat to a people who are often hungry.

6. *Means of Livelihood*

Pastoralists by inclination, the Murle are only agriculturists by necessity, but even within the narrow confines of their world, climatic conditions vary considerably and so affect their way of life. In the hilly country round Boma the soil is more fertile and the rainfall heavier, so that in a good year three crops may be grown. The presence of tsetse fly, however, prevents the keeping of cattle there; bridewealth therefore consists of sheep and goats, and the bridegroom has to work in the cultivation of his parents-in-law.

The sandier soils of the Veveno in the west are better for cattle, and there many of the Ngarotti lead an almost entirely pastoral life, hardly cultivating at all, but living off the milk and blood of their cattle, and on fish, game, and the roots and berries they can find locally.

On the heavier clays of the main river a more mixed economy is followed. Early ripening maize and tobacco are grown in small plots round the homesteads, and large fields, enclosed by thorn hedges to protect them from the ravages of game animals, are planted with several varieties of millet. These are all sown together as a form of insurance, because different weather conditions suit different varieties. Other crops include gourds and pumpkins, and sometimes a little sesame and groundnuts, although these are mainly grown on Boma to provide fats.

Agriculture, cooking, and housebuilding are mainly the work of the married women, each of whom has her own hut and field. Husbands help their wives with the heavier jobs of clearing trees and bushes from the cultivations, cutting rafters for huts, and with the heavy hoeing at sowing time to clear the weeds, but the fields are owned by the women and the crops are theirs. Fishing is a mixed occupation in which all take part, and hunting and herding the cattle are men's work.

For the Murle, however, cattle are the basis of the philosophy of life. They breed cattle, marry with them, eat their meat, drink their blood and milk, and sleep on their hides. Their old songs are full of references to the lowing of herds captured from their neighbours in battle. For young and old, men and women, cattle provide the most absorbing topic of conversation. Young men live with the cattle all the year, searching for grazing and guarding the herds against harm from man or beast. Even when they talk about girls they cannot keep off the subject of cattle, for flirting leads to marriage and this involves the transference of cattle. The old men settling disputes at the village clubs do so in terms of cattle, because they have to be paid in compensation or atonement. Women preparing food for their families discuss milk yields as they churn butter. Cattle are known and loved individually, and when they die they are believed to join the spirits of their ancestors. Every important social event is celebrated by sacrifice, to ensure the participation of the ancestral spirits as well as to provide food for the assembled guests and relatives. Kinship obligations are expressed in terms of cattle, as is the strength of feeling between 'best friends' in their exchange of animals as gifts. Wealth means the possession of many cattle, and poverty the lack of them. When the head of a homestead dies, his corpse is laid in the centre of the enclosure, that the herd may take leave of its late master, so close is their identification with cattle, which are also extremely important in their religious beliefs.

With such an overriding interest in these animals it is not

surprising that there is a considerable vocabulary of cattle terms.[1]
There are special words for every colour and colour combination;
for cows and calves, bulls and oxen, at every stage of their growth;
for different kinds of horns and for all the conformations to which
their horns can be trained to grow—an art in which they take the
greatest interest and pride. Frequently they throw up their arms
in imitation of the shape of an animal's horns when discussing them,
and every young man is given an ox by his father or uncle when
he reaches man's estate. He spends hours singing to his special
ox, from which he takes his bull name; the ox learns to recognize
his master's voice, and a strange bond grows up between man and
beast.

To bleed their cattle they tie the neck of the selected beast to
make the jugular vein swell, and then shoot a small arrow from
a bow into the vein. The operation is not difficult for a man who
is adept at handling his cattle, but the Murle cannot explain why
this method is always employed, and it is the only use to which
they put bows and arrows. It was from this custom that Driberg
drew the title of his book on the Didinga.[2] Every homestead has
its own bow and arrow, and cattle are bled about once in six weeks.
The blood is collected in a gourd, and sometimes drunk at once,
if the need is great; but usually it is allowed to dry into a thick
black pudding, or mixed with milk into a paste.

The Murle live off their cattle, but they also live with them.
The organization of their daily activities is planned round cattle,
and so with much of their social activity, because the conditions
of the country are such that a semi-nomadic life is necessary to
secure sufficient grazing and water at all times of the year. The
young bloods in the warrior grade, the pride of the race, give up
the comforts of home life for a wandering existence in the rudest
of temporary shelters, and the entire life of the tribe is bound up
with the well-being of its herds to such an extent that, while cattle
are an economic necessity and the main source of livelihood, they
are also something more, supplying a spiritual need of the people
whose lives they share so closely. Young boys milk them in the
morning and the warriors in the evening, the girls helping on both
occasions. Older people help by collecting dung for the fires which
are essential to keep off flies and mosquitoes at night. When a

[1] See Appendix B.
[2] J. H Driberg, *The People of the Small Arrow*, Routledge, London, 1930.

young man wishes to marry, he looks to his father and his mother's relatives to provide the marriage cattle. When these are transferred to the girl's homestead, they are divided amongst her relatives, so that people who are related are spoken of as *atenoc*—literally 'there are cattle between them'. When cattle leave one homestead and enter another, they have to be ceremonially blessed by the head of the new homestead to ensure that no ill befalls them or the cattle already there. This rite, known as *bulanet*, may provide a clue to the name of the clan to which the chiefs belong, Bulanec. For the ceremony, which is performed on the central mound in the middle of the homestead, known as *kuwet*,[1] most clans use coffee beans ground up with charcoal and ash from the dung fires, which is rubbed on to the cow's back by the head of the homestead. The blessing of the cattle, *toven*,[2] is a sign of their identification with their new homestead, and illustrates their religious importance to the Murle.

Sheep and goats provide an important supplement to the cattle economy, invaluable both for food and minor sacrifices. The customary repayment for the use or loan of a large ram is a bull calf; this link enables a hard-working man to acquire cattle and eventually become rich. By assiduous hunting and fishing a man can make presents of meat, which one day will be paid for in sheep or goats. A successful hunter who sells his meat to the hungry Anuak in exchange for tobacco, which they grow in quantity, can make a good profit, because tobacco always fetches a high price, in terms of sheep and goats, within the tribe. If he can grow a large surplus of grain or tobacco, this too can be sold for sheep: other people make articles such as baskets, stools, and various containers, with goats as the medium of exchange. In these ways a flock of sheep and goats can be accumulated and gradually exchanged for cattle. Small boys are taught the duties of herding by being put in charge of flocks of sheep and goats, which, as it were, provide the 'small change' of the cattle economy.

7. *Hunting*

In addition to this herding, the Murle are extremely skilful in the arts of hunting and stalking game. They make several different kinds of traps and snares, train their dogs to help them, and build fences to force the game when driven to take special paths, where

[1] Cf. p. 41.   [2] Cf. pp. 16, 60.

huntsmen await them. The country is well stocked with game, for which they have a very extensive vocabulary, and the meat thus obtained forms an important part of their diet. Hunting goes on all through the year, but it is the annual game migration from the south after the rains that provides most meat, although the game returning southwards in the early rains also pays a heavy toll. At this time of the year the game tires easily, owing to the heavy going, but it is generally more scattered than during the north-wards migration in December. This starts in the mountains of Uganda, one branch coming past Mount Kathiangor and up the River Kengen, which is crossed at a ford a few miles south of Pibor Post, and known to the Murle as 'the tree of meat'. The annual slaughter, mostly of thiang, oribi, white-eared cob, and various gazelles, is very considerable, as the herds keep on moving northwards in the same area for several days on end. Much of this meat is dried into biltong and kept for later use. The young men cut off the ears of the game they kill, the left or right ear according to which side the animal was speared, and hang them up on their mothers' huts. A young man with several of these trophies is very proud, and earns the praises of the girls for being a real man. The hind legs of animals killed hunting are reserved for the elders at the club,[1] and any young man who failed to pay them their due would be liable to the fine of a goat. There are elaborate rules for the distribution of all meat, both game killed hunting and cattle or sheep slaughtered at ceremonies.

Hunting dangerous animals such as lion, leopard, elephant, buffalo, and rhinoceros is one of the few ways left in which the young men can still prove their manliness and courage. For this they invoke the aid of the chiefs, who are endowed with power to bless them, and wave their sacred *giina* spears in the direction in which the animals are thought to be, in much the same way as in times of war.[2] For this assistance the chiefs are entitled to hunting dues: an elephant's tusk, a leopard's skin, and the foreleg of a giraffe or buffalo. The hides of the last two are used for making shields; leopard skins are traditionally the prerogative of chiefs, and ivory is, of course, valuable for making bracelets and for trading with the Anuak. When an elephant is killed, the owner of the first spear, *et c'aminto*, takes both tusks, one for himself and one for his chief. The owner of the second spear is known as *et ci*

---

[1] Cf. p. 38.   [2] Cf. p. 68.

ladinto. The constellation of the plough is called 'the commoner's elephant'; the three stars of the handle being the owners of the first and second spears, and the *et ci beo* the owner of the stone on which the huntsmen's spears were sharpened.

The Murle also have an expert knowledge of woodcraft, and the endurance of the young men on hunting parties, often with the minimum of food for several days, is remarkable. Because their country is better stocked with game than that of the Nuer or Dinka, this factor strikes one forcibly as a significant difference between neighbouring tribes living in similar conditions. An incident which occurred a few years ago is typical of their attitude towards hunting: some young men, stung by the taunts of their elders that they were not the braves their fathers had been in their youth, stalked a buffalo, roped it, and dragged it back to the club to prove their prowess to the astonished elders, with the rejoinder 'At least you never did that in your youth.'

8. *Fishing*

Fish also provide an important ingredient of their diet. Fish-traps are set in the long grass at the edges of the rivers all through the year, and when they are falling, fish-weirs are built at strategic points to prevent the fish escaping from the well-known pools. These are owned by particular clans, and the man who represents the clan's rights is called the man (or owner) of the pool, *et ci lelo*. He is really more the spiritual guardian, responsible for carrying out the proper ceremonies before fishing starts, than the legal owner of the pool, because it is thought that the season's fishing would be poor if the due ceremony had not been performed. He fixes the day for fishing to start, after consultation with the leading elders and the local chief. Enormous crowds gather on the appointed day, which, in the case of the large pools, usually falls in April or May. The men and boys are armed with fish-spears and hooks on short sticks, and the women and girls with large baskets. The men go ahead, stabbing right and left, and the women with their leather skirts tucked between their legs and into their belts, form a line across the pool, plunging their baskets down to the bottom as they wade from end to end. The process is repeated time after time and, by the day's end, large numbers of fish are caught. The surplus is dried in the sun, and is extremely valuable provender while the new grain is growing and the last season's crop almost exhausted.

All the important pools have their own songs and rites, but Nyandit[1] ('great crocodile' to the Nuer and Dinka), which belongs to the Longarim, on the main river, is regarded as the most important, and the shrine there, a great pile of sticks under the bank at the water's edge, is known as 'God's House'. Here live bulls are sacrificed, whereas at other pools the offering is only of sheep and goats. Every passer-by is supposed to add a stick to the shrine, which is liberally decorated with women's beads and small iron rings. Nobody should approach this shrine without first washing himself all over, and no one would dare cut wood from the thicket surrounding the shrine. This pool is regarded with the greatest awe; and its guardian, Madhi Piriatoddo, derives considerable respect as well as profit from his position, for no man would fish there without first giving him a small present—a ring or bracelet, or some tobacco or grain. Some of these gifts Madhi throws into the pool for the benefit of the spirits, but others he keeps for his own use.

It is said that when cattle are sacrificed there they are pushed into the pool alive, and never come up again. Visiting Nuer scornfully explained this to me by saying that the mud at the bottom of the pool was very sticky and clinging, and that the beasts were caught in it and then eaten by crocodiles. Madhi naturally maintains that they are taken by the spirits of the pool. As the special song for this pool, like many others, could not be translated by themselves, it suggests a foreign element and probably means the shrine has been taken over from previous Dinka owners.

In addition to the owners of these pools, there are a few crocodile experts, *et c'agul*, whose services are employed to ensure safety when the pool in question is fished. Wercum Lopillap, one of the most noted crocodile experts, was a friend of mine, and one day in April 1943 I went with him for the start of the fishing in Lottipongo pool. Gogol, then chief of the area, had fixed the day, and the owner of the pool, Annol Ngaico, had made the customary offerings of grain and tobacco the previous night, and sacrificed a goat under the grass fringing the pool. We arrived there shortly before dawn and Wercum immediately went to the edge of the water, a very long narrow strip in the bed of the river, and stooping

[1] Cf. p. 60.

down picked up a lump of mud from the reeds at the water's
edge. He then turned and asked for a ring, which was given by one
of the spectators. He proceeded to make a model crocodile with
the mud. Considerable care was taken over this, and the final
product, some ten inches long, was quite a good likeness, but had
a very large mouth, in which the ring, firmly closed, was embedded;
the mouth was also closed, and Wercum was ready to begin his
part of the ceremony. He advanced alone into the water until it
reached his knees, cleared a space in the grass at the edge of the
pool, tying a piece of grass round his waist, stooped down, and
pushed the image into the mud. He then harangued the pool,
invoking his father and ancestors, and told the pool that if anything
was there it was not to bite but to stay where it was quietly. He
stooped again, cupped his hands, scooped water into the air, so that
it fell on the waiting crowd at the water's edge, turned and did
the same to the river, turned again, and repeated the process to
the crowd, saying 'May you live!' With a loud shout of 'Live!',
everyone rushed into the water and fishing began. No one was hurt
that day, but the following afternoon a fair-sized crocodile was
killed without injury to anyone. Wercum's stock was high and his
own pleasure undisguised.

As most political power is concentrated in the hands of the
drumchiefs, the influence of ritual experts is small by comparison,
although the emphasis laid on correct procedure by all members
of the tribe is illustrated in their attitude to these experts, all of
whom are rewarded for the part they play in their appropriate
functions.

9. *Organization of Villages*

During the rains the whole tribe lives in the semi-permanent
villages on the higher ground along the rivers. For the rest of the
year, as we have seen, the warriors and most of the cattle are
away in temporary camps, *bul*, living a life of their own. The older
people and children move into temporary quarters too, with a few
milch cows, but only for a few months of the year, during the hot
weather when there is little else for them to do. They usually
move in December after the game migration is over, and by March
or April are starting to move back to prepare the ground for cultivation and to repair their houses. They are only away from the
villages for three or four months, in contrast to the warriors who

spend but three or four months in them at the height of thé wet season. It is, therefore, difficult to describe their territorial distribution because they are always on the move, according to the seasons of the year, and their movements in one year do not always correspond with those of the next, owing to variation in rainfall. In dry years, when water supplies have become limited by the dry-weather period, the concentration on certain large pools is greater than in wetter years. Normally, however, all the herds of a village or district tend to join up towards the end of the dry weather. Even then the village people do not join the warriors but make their temporary homesteads, *korok ci tagethu*, which are replicas in miniature of the permanent homesteads, *korok ci lorecu*, whenever they find a convenient spot not too far from their village. It is only during the heavy rains that the whole tribe lives in the villages, and then social life is at its height.

These village communities consist of groups of homesteads sited together within a defined territorial area, and sharing in the activities organized at the village clubs. They may consist of anything from two or three homesteads to as many as twenty or more, and often straggle for several miles along the banks of one of the rivers. Their layout is haphazard, according to the chance distribution of mounds or eminences on which the homesteads are built against flooding during the rains. Their boundaries are well known, a dry watercourse, a clump of trees, or some other suitable landmark serving to divide one village from another. The people of a village form a community and are referred to as such: for instance, *ol ci* Maintakaro means 'the people of Maintakaro's village', by way of distinction from those of any other village.

Membership of the village community is symbolically conferred on a new homestead that wishes to join by the *et ci toddo* giving the newcomers a lighted brand with which to light their first fire in their new home. For this service he will later expect a present of meat, when one of the newcomers has been successful out hunting. The term *et ci toddo* may be translated as 'the man of the land' or the 'owner of the ground', who is invariably a descendant of the first settler in the area. He is not so much the owner—for the Murle say that all land belongs to the chiefs—as the ritual expert who has to perform the appropriate ceremonies at seed time and harvest to ensure the success of the crops of his village. His functions are regarded as of little importance in Lotilla, but are taken far more seriously on Boma, where agriculture is the main source of livelihood.

10. *The Clubs*

It is the clubs which provide a focus for village life, and a centre where those social activities which the homestead cannot provide for its members are planned and organized. A club is known as *ri*, literally 'the shade', from the large shady tree under which the elders sit and gossip, with the *baal* or dancing floor beside it. The elders of a village spend most of the day there talking, arguing, settling disputes, and smoking. Dances, of course, bring the whole community together at the club, but if one of the warrior age-sets wishes to hold a dance, permission of the elders must first be obtained at the club, for it is a village activity which entails the preparation of food. The settlement of a serious dispute or the planning of an important fishing expedition may attract quite a number of interested people, but on ordinary days the club provides a meeting-place for the elders, who are probably joined by the middle-aged men later in the morning when they have finished their work in the cultivations or homesteads.

The elders spend the whole day there, only breaking up at sunset to return home for their evening meal, and their greatest pleasure in life is in smoking their pipes at the club. These consist of small wooden bowls on a stem which is fixed into a large gourd with a long mouthpiece: the gourd is half-filled with water, to which is added grains of millet. The smoke is drawn bubbling through this mixture, the tobacco being lighted by placing a glowing ember or a piece of charcoal over the bowl. In time the mixture inside the gourd grows rich, and a Murle elder smoking has to be seen to be believed. After a few puffs he starts to choke and splutter, and frequently has to call for a drink of water to recover his breath. It is not considered good manners to keep the pipe for more than a few minutes at a time, and so it is kept circulating amongst those present. So great is their craving for tobacco that there is a special phrase for a 'tobacco-less world', *amum loici*, and the usual term for a human being is *et ci der*, the owner of a pipe.

11. *The Village*

When discussing the organization of their villages the Murle say that 'People are many, like *lamurwac*' or 'The people have spread like *lamurwac'*. This refers to the grass *Cynodon dactylon* which grows on the mounds on which their homesteads are built. This simile is also used in connection with kinship, referring to the kinship links formed by marriages between members of the different homesteads living in the village. The phrase is very apt, because this grass grows in small clumps that send out runners in every direction, which, in turn, put down roots and form fresh clumps, until the ground is covered by a thick mat of criss-crossing runners.

It is the cross-cutting of kinship ties between the constituent homesteads of a village which, reinforced by the ties of friendship, common interests, and shared activities, gradually bind them together into a community. For although an individual family is free to move to another village, and frequently does so for a variety of reasons, such as poor crops, sickness in the herds, quarrels, and, more particularly, the death of the head of the homestead, once this homestead has been accepted into a village community it will probably return there at some time in the future. In this way, village communities, although they often change from year to year, nevertheless tend to persist over the years. The Murle stress the importance of this web of kinship ties, binding them together, because they are usually more interested in the links between living people than in their descent groups, clans, and lineages, which supply kinship links between their ancestors. This shows a natural and healthy interest in the present, and the network of a village provides the important links in their everyday social life, although the patrilineal lineage system is more important in the tribal structure and in connection with the marriage of an individual. Although the Murle argue that members of a clan should live together where the clan has rights in cultivable land or water, in fact many people prefer to live with other relatives or friends. 'The clans have scattered' they say, but admit that they were always so, although less markedly in the past, when the need of one's clansmen's support was more frequently needed.

In 1942 Tambet village, which I knew well because of its proximity to Pibor Post, consisted of eight homesteads. By 1948 only four of these remained there, although six homesteads which were regarded as members of the Tambet village group were living in Kavacoc, the next village, in order to be further away from the Police Post. Ngaici, the head of one of the homesteads, had died in 1944, and his son had moved as a sign of mourning to Kalbat that year, and back again in 1947 to Kavacoc. Awutok, the head of another homestead, had also died, and his homestead subsequently split in two, one son moving with part of the family to Maintakar and the other half staying in Tambet. Two other homesteads had left, but others that had formerly been members of the community had returned, so that, including the Tambet homesteads living just over the Kavacoc boundary, the village community consisted of ten homesteads in 1948 compared with eight in 1942.

An investigation of three villages on the Veveno revealed ten homesteads in Veveno Teden, comprising 102 souls: 32 men, 35 women, 25 boys, and 10 girls; an average of 10·2 people in a homestead. The fourteen homesteads of Yor village housed 159 people in 53 huts: 50 men, 54 women, 30 boys, and 25 girls; an average of 11·2 persons per homestead. Ngaiciveraicidh village comprised twelve hamlets housing 173 people in 62 huts: 53 men, 62 women, 33 boys, and 25 girls. The average here, of 14·5, was higher because the village included the exceptionally large homestead of Apul Kimma, one of the richest men in the tribe; his homestead was virtually a hamlet in itself. Homesteads of this size are very rare, the normal range being anything from six to twenty-five or thirty persons. In the same way, although there are a number of small villages with only two or three homesteads, most contain between ten and twenty.

12. *Homesteads*[1]

The Murle maintain that in the past the number of both village communities and the occupants of a homestead were greater than today, because of their fear of attack and the need for collective defence.

The homestead is the basic unit of social and economic life. It consists of a group of huts arranged in a rough circle, linked together by thorn hedges to provide protection for the cattle, which are kraaled in the centre of the enclosure at night. Small patches of tobacco on the outside of the circle are also fenced in, although the main cultivations are usually separate from the living quarters and often a considerable distance away. The hut of the

---

[1] Cf. the dispersed hamlets of Nuer and Dinka, and p. 102.

senior wife is always at Jen, the place of honour to the east, for
they say the layout of their homesteads symbolizes the migrations
of the tribe: this can be seen in the following diagram:[1]

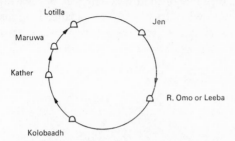

When discussing a homestead they also speak of it as having
four horns or corners, and regard the rough circle formed by the
surrounding fence as being divided into four segments. These are
ngum, the forehead or front, to the east, with *zugum* or back
opposite, to the west; to the north is the left side and to the south
the right side. The first, corresponding to Jen, is the segment of
the senior wife, *ngai cen abu*; her hut is built, not due east of the
central fires, but in the northern corner of her segment. In the
next is that of the second wife, *ngai ci kanowaan*, whose hut is
built at the eastern corner of the southern segment. In the third
segment is that of the third wife, or if there are more than four,
the intermediate wives, *ngai ci korgenya*—the senior of these
would build her hut in the south of the western segment. Finally,
the junior wife, *ngai ci totur*, who is also known as *ngai ci vorunta*,
the wife 'who came afterwards', or the wife of the stool, *ngai ci
lecer*, because it is her particular duty to look after her husband in
his old age, has the northern segment, with her hut in the western
part.

When I first understood this conception of the homestead and
drew it on the ground they laughed their assent. They then drew
in the double line linking the two entrances to the homestead and
asked if I knew what the point of intersection in the centre represented: I was told that it was the 'place of power', *kuwet*, the site
of the fire, or the place of blessing,[2] where the head of the homestead blesses the cattle. *Kuwet* also means the top of the head, and
in practice is used to mean the place of power and influence. It is

[1] Cf. pp. 19, 48, and 102.　　　　[2] Cf. pp. 16, 60.

doubtful if many homesteads exactly reproduce this pattern on the
ground, but the idea is important to the Murle because it demon-
strates the ideal which every man hopes to attain in his old age:
it is a typical example of their dualistic way of regarding the whole
as being composed of two pairs in balanced opposition. Their
word for this is *venon*, the term *aveno* being used to express
objects of thought in opposition or contrast.[1]

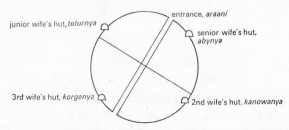

In spite of the fact that homesteads seldom correspond to this
ideal, it governs their layout in particular. There is only one fixed
point of reference, that of the senior wife's hut at Jen, those of the
other married women being arranged in their order of precedence
within the family group. If any hut is out of place there is always
good reason in explanation, and individual homesteads naturally
vary according to the relationships of those who live therein. This
exposition, based on the rules of family seniority, with the cattle
kraaled in the centre but near the hut of the owner, is typical, as
is the symbolical layout conforming to their migrations, and both
are part of the associations of the word *korok*, here translated as
'homestead'. The word literally means the dung fires in the centre
of the enclosure, which are lit every night to ward off mosquitoes
and other insects that torment the cattle. By association it comes to
be applied to the huts and byres within the kraal and its surrounding fence, as well as the people who live there as a social and
economic group: it is a word pregnant with meaning for the Murle.
The small homesteads of two or three huts to be found in every
village are regarded as the beginnings of the large homestead
which every man would like to gather round him in his old age.
When these ambitions are achieved, one kraal is often insufficient,
and subsidiary enclosures are built on to the main circle; even then,
the position of the various huts conforms to the accepted pattern.

[1] Cf. pp. 16, 42, 47, 102, and *Symbols of Unity*, Ch. VII, § 13.

13. *Huts*

Murle huts are extremely primitive and generally described as 'beehive'. They are built by the women with a minimum of assistance from their menfolk. A bride is given an axe by her family on marriage for the purpose of building her hut. The kidney-shaped living huts, *ciedh*, are built in two parts, the round living-room first, and afterwards the porch, *rom*. Sticks are firmed into the ground and bound together with strips of *yoey* bark into a framework. When this is about five and a half feet high it is bent inwards and branches are tied across the top to make a roof. The main support poles are called *kittir*, and the rafters tied to them *merrel*. The opening into the porch is known as the 'hut's throat', *ciedh ellem*; the doorway, *tatok*, which is closed with a door, *karogi*, leads to the porch. The whole framework, seldom exceeding seven feet at the highest point, is thatched with bundles of grass tied on with *yoey* bark. The women collect the grass in large bundles, which they carry back on their heads, using the skins they wear on the upper part of their bodies as a head pad while doing so.

There is little variation in the internal arrangements of the huts. The most important part, because it is the coolest and darkest, is the *totomot* behind the entrance to the main hut, where distinguished visitors are housed, because there they will be least bothered by flies. Opposite this may be the enclosure for sheep and goats, and sometimes calves, *teny*. In the centre of the floor of the main hut is the fireplace, formed of three or four mud blocks, *kidhinga*. On one side of this is the woman's bed, *caf caf*, made of long sticks tied together and covered with a skin, while on the opposite side there is a raised platform, *kerca*, where the young children sleep. Adult girls usually sleep on skins in the porch.

This group normally comprises a polygamous family living together under the leadership of the *et ci kurgo* or head of the homestead, whose position in society is of considerable importance. It is he who directs the family's activities, which are shared according to age and sex: the women fetch water, cook food, cultivate crops, and in their spare time sit in the appointed place, *rerum*, where they eat their evening meal together. Similarly the men have their own sitting-out place, *lettem*, generally under a tree, and outside the thorn fence if there is no suitable tree within the enclosure. The young men graze the family cattle as a single herd, and the head of the homestead disposes of particular beasts as he thinks best

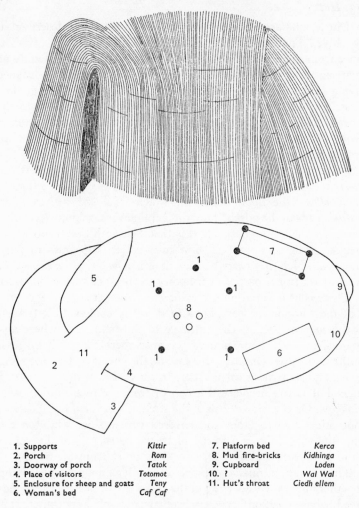

1. Supports	*Kittir*	7. Platform bed	*Kerca*
2. Porch	*Rom*	8. Mud fire-bricks	*Kidhinga*
3. Doorway of porch	*Tatok*	9. Cupboard	*Loden*
4. Place of visitors	*Totomot*	10. ?	*Wal Wal*
5. Enclosure for sheep and goats	*Teny*	11. Hut's throat	*Ciedh ellem*
6. Woman's bed	*Caf Caf*		

for the general good, although each one is owned by a family or individual within the group. In the same way, he represents any member of the homestead who is concerned in a dispute before the village elders. If evil befalls the homestead, all the fires are extinguished, and it is he who lights a new one with the sacred firesticks inherited from his father. In order to prevent witchcraft everybody in any way connected with the homestead has to walk over this fire, for it is thought that anyone who has cast a spell on it would be too afraid of incurring ill effects if he did so. Other articles inherited by the head of a homestead from his father, and passed on to his heir, are a special spear used at marriages for the division of cattle, and a gourd from which he sprinkles water on the disputants when he has settled a family quarrel.

14. *Education of Children*

As soon as they are old enough, children help their parents, and often elder brothers and sisters, in their appointed tasks, and in this way receive much of their practical education. So marked is the division of labour between the sexes that on the birth of a child a neighbour will ask 'Is it something that will go to the river?', and the reply, if it is a boy, will be 'No. Something which will go to the club.' A considerable amount of moral education is given to children by their parents. They are taught to respect their elders, to be polite and listen to what they are told, and not to insult, for fear of being cursed; they are taught to be truthful, and warned that if they acquire the reputation of lying it will count against them in later life, in such cases as the division of cattle after a raid, or meat after hunting. Stealing and greediness are frowned upon, and a child who repeatedly steals food will have his hands scalded with boiling porridge to teach him a lesson, and will be taunted with aping a hyena, *gudholoc*.

When a girl reaches marriageable age, a reputation for being good-natured, a careful worker, and a good cook, is a valuable asset, for such qualities will influence future mothers-in-law far more than good looks. Generosity is encouraged, especially to a relative in distress, because it is regarded as a great virtue; at the same time, however, children are warned to look after the family property diligently and see that it is not wasted. Fathers tell their sons to mark their words, encouraging them to strive to the utmost when fishing or hunting, while being careful not to wound a companion with spear or fish-hook. An old man's greatest joy is to sit at the club and watch his son jumping at a dance or practising fighting. He is overjoyed if his son's bravery or skill is commented upon favourably after a hunt, for bravery is the greatest of the virtues, respect for one's elders the hallmark of good behaviour, and a reputation for truthfulness and generosity universally desired.

III

THE DRUMSHIPS AND THE
TRIBAL STRUCTURE

THE Murle still claim that there are four drumships, *kidong-wana en wec*, and although strictly this is not now true, it is clear that they mean there should be four. At present the Kelenya and Ngenvac have lost their drums, and as a result are losing all political influence, while both the Tangajon and Ngarotti drums have 'split', as they say. When judgement is announced at the end of important cases, the names of the four drumships are still invoked, although in reality the organization of the tribe now consists of two Tangajon drumships, with whom the Kelenya go, on the one hand, balanced by the two Ngarotti drumships, with the Ngenvac, on the other.

I have advisedly translated the term *kidongwa* (pl. *kidongwana*) as 'drumships' for two reasons: first, the word is derived from the word *kidong*, meaning a drum; and second, I do not find drumship easy to define further, although this appears to be no problem for the Murle. With them a drumship is interpreted quite simply in kinship terms, as a lineage of the chiefly Bulanec clan and its attached commoner clans. It is, however, also a territorial unit with clearly defined boundaries, and so may be said to consist of a group of villages all in one area, with their appropriate grazing lands; and thus 'drumship' might also be called 'district'. I suspect also that in days gone by, when the military organization occupied a more dominant position in society, that the drumship may well have been referred to as a 'regiment', drawing its recruits from particular clans in a distinct area.

The Murle insist that all the land belongs to the chiefs and that the land of any one of the drumships belongs to a particular branch of the Bulanec clan. They explain that when the Lotilla valley was conquered from the Dinka some five to six generations ago the chiefs divided the land between them. In fact, it was the rivers they divided, from the central point of Mount Lothir some fifteen miles west of Pibor Post, and this division still stands. They treated the river system of the Lotilla valley as forming a rough circle, and divided it into four segments,[1] the junior Tangajon drumship 'going with' the Kelenya, and taking the north-east segment; the senior Tangajon taking their rightful place to the south-east; the Ngaicimut Ngarotti taking their stand to the south-west, followed by a small patch for the Ngenvac; while the Ngaloaga Ngarotti swing in a wide arc from the south-west to the Tangajon boundaries in the north-east. Diagramatically the division may be expressed as follows:

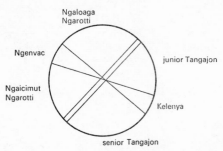

The diagram, however, has had to be 'stretched' to conform to the actual geographical distribution of the river system with which they were faced, as perhaps the map on page 48 will show, as well as to the historical fact that the Kelenya and Ngenvac had lost their drums. The importance of their principle of *venon*[2] is illustrated once again in this territorial layout of their drumship.

In kinship terms the Kelenya used to be the *abunya* or senior drumship, the Tangajon the *kanowanya*, the Ngarotti the *korgenya*, and the Ngenvac, probably taking the place of the lost Longarim, the *toturnya*; and although, as described in the previous chapter, they live in semi-nomadic village communities which are not constant, their permanent organization is expressed in terms of clans.

I referred to this point in the Introduction, because, although this division of society into two halves is considered important by the Murle, in everyday life I failed to observe that it made any difference whether a man belonged to the Bulanec (a name with cattle-owning overtones) or the Celi (with hunting associations)— except in the hearing of cases. Then, indeed, the chiefs and all the Bulanec clan sat on one side and the commoners on the other, and for this reason I consider their emphasis on the distinction in conversation today is a reflection of its historical importance

[1] Cf. p. 151.   [2] Cf. pp. 16, 42, 102, and Symbols of Unity, Ch. VII, § 13.

handed down over the generations. It may well refer to the fusion
long ago of a copper-skinned, cattle-owning aristocracy with a
dark-skinned race of hunters, although they do not regard it in
this light, maintaining that they were all created at one and the

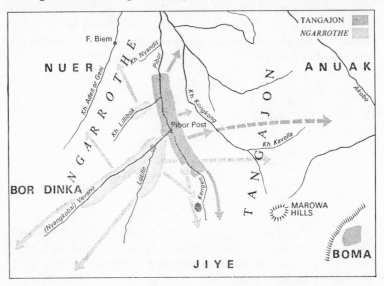

same time at Jen.[1] For them it is another instance of the balance of
opposites. There are two traditions: one that at one time they had
no cattle but used to tame wild animals, *abal kelek*, and another
that cattle were created at Jen with the original Murle; although
they realize the two beliefs are inconsistent they are at a loss to
explain them. The Bulanec are spoken of as red chiefs, *alaat ci
meirik*, as opposed to the black people or commoners, *ol ci kolik*
or *celi*, a word which means 'hunter' and is derived from *cel*,
'hunting'; the chiefs and their close relatives may not eat honey,
a delicacy which is enjoyed by all others.

If one asks a Murle, as I frequently did, to which clan he belongs,
he will amost invariably say 'Bulanec' or 'Celi', whichever is
appropriate. To a repeated request he gives the name of his drumship, and it is only at the third time of asking that he gives his clan.
Of many Bulanec they say 'They are only ordinary Bulanec, not
chiefs', *Bulanec labak lang en alaat*, implying that they are so
distantly related that they would not perform any functions of the

[1] Cf. pp. 19, 41.

drumchiefs. They are the descendants of junior lineages which branched off from the parent stem so long ago that the point of contact with the senior line has been forgotten. Some clans considered as commoners today may well at one time have been junior branches of the Bulanec. The Tangko clan in the Ngarotti drumship is possibly a case in point, which would account for their association with the Ngarotti—'going with it' as they say; this is borne out by the fact that the Tangko do not have to surrender leopard skins to the chiefs, and are said to have been allowed to keep the slaves they captured in the past when they went to war. When a commoner-clan is mentioned people generally know to which drumship it belongs, except in the case of a small or little-known clan.

The Murle's explanation of their structure in terms of clans and drumships is therefore correct, but it is not a complete explanation of the position today, because other factors are involved. Observation shows that the drumships are territorial units within village communities; some villages are, however, associated with particular commoner-clans, usually the clan of the first settler from which the man of the land is descended. It is in this sense that the pattern of the drumships still corresponds in their eyes with the ideal pattern of the homestead.

1. *Kelenya Drumship*

Despite the loss of their drum the Kelenya still have the proud claim of being the senior branch of the Bulanec, and one of their songs includes the line *Ken abu naana*, 'I am the senior'. They have pride of place and are therefore given priority. The name Kelenya is said to be derived from the word *kelang*, which means a leopard; it is perhaps significant that the senior branch of the Bulanec should be known by this name, for leopard skins are traditionally associated with these chiefs and the skins of all leopards killed have to be given to the chief of the killer. In the past the Kelenya drumchief is said always to have worn a leopard skin and to have made his followers wear leopard-skin tassels. In Murle thought, wearing a leopard skin implies being 'mantled with the night sky', because the same colour-conformation *budhen* is applied to a spotted leopard skin and to the star-spangled night sky,[1] and thus it follows that calling the followers of the senior drumchief 'the leopard people' has grandiloquent overtones for the tribe.

[1] Cf. p. 90.

Another story confirming the seniority of the Kelenya is their association with rats. In 1942 there was a plague of rats throughout the country, and I was told that they had come to mourn Maraka, the Kelenya chief who died in 1940. They believe that rats always come to mourn a Kelenya chief, and, more particularly, the mother of a chief,[1] and say that they are the peculiar property of the Kelenya 'like dogs with other people'. It is said that if the Kelenya chief was annoyed with somebody in the past he would catch a rat and send it to bite the offender, who would probably die as the wound would turn septic. To this day the Kelenya are supposed to smear some fat on the nose of any rat they find eating their grain, give it a little grass, and tell it to go away and live in the bush. The connection with the myth of the creation described on page 20 is clearly recognized by the Murle.

Today the Kelenya have only five villages: Kelenya and Walaak on the west bank; Cindur, Gidhain, and Lokoli on the east of the river. Most of the members of commoner-clans associated with this drumship are living dispersed in Tangajon or Ngarotti territory; these are Riaka, Maintang, Martok, Tenu, Dhowe, Agoi, Maintamma, and Girocol: the last-named are said not to be bitten by mosquitoes.

The small size of this drumship is always attributed to the loss of their drum and the casualties sustained by them in previous generations in their wars against the Anuak. The drum was lost five generations ago when Maindo was killed by the Tapotha at Mount Kumkumen in the Maruwa hills. This is their traditional centre, where many of their chiefs are supposed to be buried, and where they are said to have had brass or copper stools. The story runs that Maindo told his young men not to attack the Tapotha, but his orders were disobeyed and the attack made. While the warriors were away the Tapotha came and attacked the defence-less Kelenya villages, carrying off many women and children and killing the aged Maindo. They did not destroy the drum because he had hidden it in a cave in the mountain, but before he died, Maindo is said to have cursed his sons for disobeying his orders. When the young men returned, his sons went out to look for the drum, but the effect of their father's curse was so great that on approaching it they became demented, and the drum is believed to be in the cave to this day.

[1] Cf. p. 21.

During the last three or four generations the Kelenya have certainly been engaged in repeated wars with the Anuak or Adonga. Three separate peace ceremonies are remembered as having been held with them. The first of these was held between Ngolotom and a certain 'Nyiju'. The last was between Maraka and Cam Akwei, the first of that name. Maraka was going to make peace with Akwei Cam, but the latter died, so he made peace with his son instead.[1] Nyijo was, in all probability, the Murle version of Cam wi Nyijuaa, in which case the Kelenya claim is supported by Anuak tradition. At this ceremony Maraka is said to have given Cam Akwei a bull, a leopard skin, and a tusk of ivory, receiving in return a bull and a girl. Maraka took a sacred *giina* spear, bent it, and ceremonially buried it as a symbol of peace between the tribes; Cam Akwei repeated the process with an Anuak spear, and a white ox was then sacrificed and eaten by both sides.

Kelenya Drumship

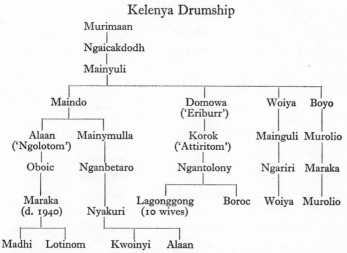

Note: The above is a simplified genealogy of the Kelenya chiefs, showing only the lines of important branches of the family.

2. *Tangajon Drumship*

The name Tangajon is said to be a nickname derived from *tangac dhodh*; the Murle say: 'If they discuss a matter, they cut the decision quickly', the inference being 'and often wrongly'.

[1] Professor E. E. Evans-Pritchard writes: 'Akwei Cam was the son of Cam wi Niyjuaa of the Nyindola lineage who was so prominent in the preceding generation' (*The Political System of the Anuak*, 1940).

They own the centre of Murleland, the Maruwa hills, and the Boma plateau far to the south-east. Here the Maijath, Vorket, Vorom, and Olginyon are regarded as drumships, although in the plains they are commoner-clans. Other large clans are the Ngatibonga, Maiyagudhul, Ngandoi, Dhoaten, Jimma, Ullo, and Lokicar, with more than twenty smaller ones. Their traditional centre, where many chiefs are said to be buried, is Mount Inidh in the Maruwa hills, although Gugu and his sister are believed to be buried at Mount Kathiangor. A vast cave in this mountain is associated with his name, as are the iron slave-rings found there by Major Darley in 1911–12.[1]

The following is the best genealogical tree I could piece together; no two chiefs agreed exactly, and many collateral lines are omitted. A long gap exists between Murimaan and Kengtidhel:

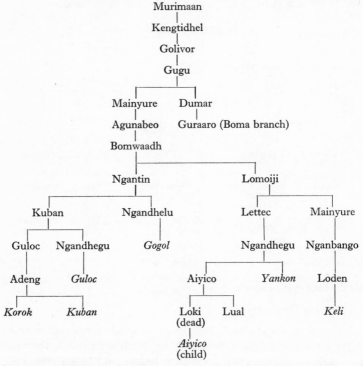

The senior branch is always referred to as the house of Ngantin and the junior as the house of Lettec, although in ordinary families

[1] Henry Darley, *Slaves and Ivory*, Witherby, London, 1926.

these would be regarded at least as *tatok*, or minimal lineages. Cattle are still exchanged between these 'houses' when daughters are married to emphasize the unity of the family. In the senior line Kuban died unmarried; a wife was therefore married to his name by Ngandhelu, who became the physical father of Guloc. In 1942 Korok Adeng, the drumchief, grandson of Guloc, was still a young man, and Gogol, legal son of Ngandhelu by his junior wife, was acting as regent for the senior Tangajon drum. By the rules of family seniority and inheritance Korok was the drumchief, but Gogol rightly expected him to pay the respect due from a nephew to his uncle, and wrongly tried to retain his position of authority at Korok's expense. This situation caused considerable difficulties for a time, but as Korok grew older he gradually assumed his rightful position in society and Gogol was forced to retire from the centre of the stage. He then settled on the east bank of the main river, and by 1949 was established as chief of seven villages north of its junction with the Kengen. Korok Adeng used to live at the large village of Tangajon, not far from Mount Lothir, where his father and grandfather are buried. All the villages between there and Maintakara were his, and his brother Kuban acts as his chief assistant. Guloc Ngandhegu had seven villages in the Turen area north of the Maruwa hills and south of the Adonga Anuak.

The territory of the junior drum, the house of Lettec, lies north of the Kelenya villages in the area known as Lilota, the lower river. It is divided into two parts by a pocket of Ngarotti territory, where Lom Cankac has two large villages, Pepper and Moincak; the cattle from these villages graze in the swamps round the Nanaam and Lilibok to the west. Yankon was chief of five villages north of Pepper, while Lual, acting as regent for his nephew Aiyico Loki, had sixteen villages south of Pepper on both sides of the river. The Tangajon graze northwards and eastwards towards the Gwom swamps and the Anuak. In the south Lettec was represented by Keili Loden, chief of seven villages in Maruwa. He was also chief of the Upper Kengen villages from which most of the Maruwa people had come. The important chiefs of the Tangajon are thus all close relatives of the two drumchiefs.

3. *The Boma Murle*

The small Boma community is really outside the scope of this account, but they do provide an interesting comparison with the

Murle of the plains on a few points, and as they are regarded as part of the Tangajon drumship, may be considered here. Korok Lokorongole, the chief, is said to be descended from Kolidhim or Guraaro, who were descended from Gugu, the great Murle chief of the Kathiangor era. Guraaro's father, Dumar, made an alliance with the Suri, who had hunting rights there, against their common enemies the Kum. He is said to have ratified the agreement by giving Guraaro's full sister to the Suri chief, saying: 'May she be fruitful and bear you children as this land will be fruitful and bear us crops.' The Boma Murle are organized in four 'drumships', although there do not seem to be clans as in the rest of the country. The Olginyon, whose name means 'the people who twist the talk', marry with the Ngalam people of Erbo in Ethiopia, and, unlike the rest of the Murle, bury their dead. Because of this the Murle call any poor man who has no cattle an *ngalamit*, and often apply the name to all the inhabitants of Boma. They have three villages, and their chief, Ibun Ngaloboli, claimed to be *mainyi ci loici*, a more pretentious term than *et ci toddo*, equivalent to 'owner of the earth' of all the land east of the Neubari river. He performs special ceremonies before sowing, and lights a new fire before people eat of the new harvest. The Olginyon have their own rain-maker, who uses coffee beans for his ceremony. The Maijath are supposed by the rest of the Murle to be peculiar—they are said to be 'few by day but many by night'. Their traditional area is Korua, west of the Neubari river. They use firesticks cut from camel's-foot trees, unlike the rest of the tribe, who use *inderab*.[1] They live mainly at Tete and Lokitiboror villages, and also bury their dead. The Vorket, the 'people of the white staves', are the descendants of those who came to Boma with Guraaro, and live at Dhingalli village, between the peaks of Towath and Ngatelewan. The Vorom, the 'people of the white ostrich feathers', live in three villages, Vorom, Nyati, and Ngalengoro, on Mount Ngatidau.

Some words used on Boma do not occur in the vocabulary of the plains Murle, and other words are pronounced differently. Nowhere else are villages so closely identified with specific clans, and homesteads are generally larger than amongst the people of the plains.

It was the Boma Murle who captured a drum from the Suri in 1934 and sent it to Korok Adeng, as heir to the senior line of the

---

[1] *Cordia abyssinica.*

family, to replace that which had been burnt by the Beir Patrol of 1912; this indicates that although there is little intercourse between the Boma community and the rest of the tribe, they still consider themselves as belonging to the Tangajon drumship.

4. *The Ngarotti Drumship*

The Ngarotti is the largest drumship and certainly the richest in cattle. This is appropriate, as their name is derived from *tang-karot*, 'the back of an ox', and they are reputed to eat the back of any bull they kill.

A common insult paid to the Ngarotti by other Murle is that they eat frogs in time of famine; they themselves boast of their numerous cattle and their military success against the Dinka. They are not considered great warriors by the rest of the tribe, who feel their successes at the expense of the Dinka were cheaply won against poor fighters, not to be compared with the Nuer, Anuak, Jiye, or Tapotha, with whom the other drumships had to contend. There are some very large commoner-clans amongst them, particularly the Mainguli, Golli, Ibbo, Tangko, Nganloki, and Anyang; the last is almost certainly of Dinka descent.

As the result of a family quarrel this drumship has also 'split': the Ngaloaga always claim to be senior to the Ngaicimut, although the latter was the senior wife. The genealogy facing page 56 illustrates the greater influence of the Ngaloaga branch at present.

Ngaicimut, the senior wife of Donge, was a very quarrelsome woman: *ngai ci moti* means the 'dangerous woman', and the village on the Veveno, Ngaiciveraicidh, is named after her. Tradition has it that she quarrelled so much with her relatives that eventually they sent her home to live with her father's people. Part of the trouble may have been due to the fact that Donge's second wife Ngaloaga had older sons than those of Ngaicimut. Some years after she had left the village Donge fell ill and sent Kelangbur—his eldest son by Ngaloaga—to bring Ngaicimut to his bedside. She refused to come. Again Donge sent his son, giving him his armpit cowbell as a sign that he was gravely ill. Kelangbur again went to Ngaicimut, and called as he was bid: 'Mother, Mother, come out, let us go'; and Ngaicimut replied: 'You, boy, what do you want from me?' He told her that he had come to fetch her before his father died, and Ngaicimut is reputed to have said: 'Do you want me because I am the senior wife? Here are the firesticks', and she threw them at him. Kelangbur picked them up, returned to his father, and related what had happened. Donge said he would bless Kelangbur; he spat on his hands, rubbed his son's face and chest, and blessed him. Then he told him to take out the grass which had been stuffed into the bell to prevent its ringing. Kelangbur did so, put the bell on, and rang it as a formal act of disinheritance of Ngaicimut's children, for Kelangbur, being the son of the second wife, was not otherwise entitled to ring the bell. His father then pointed to a special tree and told Kelangbur to make a second drum from it (the first was still with Ngaicimut). He also told him to prepare a skin for his burial and intimated where he wished his body to lie. Kelangbur did as his father commanded and covered the drum with the hide of a captured bull. It was then wrapped up in a leopard skin so that the people should not see it. Shortly afterwards Donge died, and the sons of Ngaicimut came to his homestead. When they arrived, Kelangbur told them they had come too late and that his father had appointed him as his heir, and then rang the bell at them. Golmer, Ngaicimut's eldest son, is then said to have composed his celebrated song:

> Listen red chief.
> Climb the mountain and hide your head.
> I have spoken my father
> I refuse: I burn to be black
> Bad is the persecution of the *kanowanya*.
> They think I am only a herdsboy
> But I am the head of the sons of Mainyadhi.
> I am fighting for my rights, father.
> Until I find wives for my children,
> Do not let the *kanowanya* harm me.
> They think I am only a herdsboy,
> But I am the forehead:
> I myself am the forehead of your children.
> Listen! I am fighting for my rights, father.
> Take something which is easy.
> The work of spears is swift.
> The stick has no fear.
> They are the weapons of war, my father.
> Yes. I am the heir of Mainyadhi.
> I have not yet finished this fight, father.
> I shall fight until I find a daughter-in-law,
> Listen, father. I am fighting for my rights.

This quarrel still affects the relations between the two Ngarotti families: they regard themselves as only *atenoc ci bandhetu*, that is families related by clan, in marked contrast to the feelings between the two branches of the Tangajon drumship. The Ngaloaga are very definitely the more powerful, although the drumchief is a minor. Following defeat by the Beir Patrol in 1912, Burnian left many of the duties of his office to his brother Ajubong, a rather sickly man most of his life. So it was Lom's branch of the family which established its authority over the Veveno villages, and today Toddoc, son of Nyebu, son of Lom, is chief of this area, although his old uncle Kengen Lom was still very much a power in the land when I was in their country. Kengen, in fact, acted as regent for the drumchief after Ajubong's death, only surrendering his position, with reluctance, when Poti Burnian grew old enough to assume his responsibilities. In his handing-over notes, Colonel Bacon described Kengen as 'the cleverest of the Beir Sheikhs'. When I knew him in his old age he was still a fine figure, well over six feet tall in spite of a pronounced stoop, with good features and a copper-coloured skin. Poti, on the other hand, was an awkward young man, heavily built and with a lumbering gait. He was not a good chief, and the quarrels between him and Kengen were a disturbing factor locally. The real drumchief is Ngapul, who counts as the legitimate son of Munang Burnian. He was still a youth, a Masango from Ethiopia by birth, captured by the Anuak and sold to the Murle for a tusk of ivory. Munang's wife adopted him because she failed to bear another son, and he, in due course, should succeed to his father's position and become drumchief of the Ngaloaga.

On the Ngaicimut side of the family the real drumchief is also a minor, Bobil, son of Kengen: Kengen's brother Beh, who is nominally regent, is so old and blind that in practice he lives in seclusion, leaving public affairs to his younger brother Kutek, whose area includes three villages, with another five under chief Longole to the west. The Lillibok villages are under Ibun Leberac and the large village of Okela near the Adonga Anuak is under Lotillem.

The Ngaloaga territory is far more extensive: Alaan Irir has four villages on the north bank of the Lotilla, and to the west of this lies the Ngenvac territory. On the north bank of the Veveno Amor Olebu has four villages and lives at Gummuruk. West of this lies Toddoi Nyebu's area, with eight villages. On the south bank of the Veveno is Poti Burnian's own district of seven villages round Loput, with Alaan Nyaranya at Mur ci Yodi, and several small villages further to the west. On the Upper Lotilla Lokidang Ajubong is chief of some ten villages on the east bank. The west bank is divided between Lelo Lokicar, with ten villages, in the north, and Lopile Ngatilan, with eight, in the south. All the grazing grounds to the west of the inhabited country belong to the Ngarotti.

5. *The Ngenvac Drumship*

The Ngenvac drumship is quite distinct from the others, in that its formation is remembered and only occurred a few generations ago. Apparently Dhorote, son of Metedhalu, was a man of the Ngandarec Murle on the River Omo, who acquired a drum there —history does not relate how—and came to settle with the Murle in Maruwa. He was adopted by a certain Karnyur of the Etiwur lineage of the Ngabilet clan, which henceforth assumed the status of chiefs. The Etiwur tried to imply that Dhorote was their slave, and this is recalled in the Ngenvac song:

> Listen children of Karnyur,
> Cattle are easy but humans are difficult,
> Not to be taken for nothing.
> Chief Maindhuben cursed the Kum until the sun went down;
> The drum is a dangerous thing;
> Tomorrow the drum will go to the tree
> [of shade where the cases are settled].

Both Dhorote and Tagolgol Maindhuben were killed by the Tapotha, and their son Ngando was killed by the Jekany Nuer in their great raid on the Maruwa hills. Opinions differ on who lost the drum, Tagolgol or his son; some say it was lost to the Kum, others that Ngando's wife hid it in a cave when fleeing from the Nuer, and that afterwards it could not be recovered because an ant-hill had covered the mouth of the cave. Whichever version is true, the fact remains that the drum has been lost, and with it, practically all the political influence of the Ngenvac. Today they own only a small area of land between the Ngaloaga and Ngaicimut territories, which includes Lawol and two other villages, as well as a small colony at Kolobeta, far to the south, on the upper Kengen, where Korok Kavula is chief.

The accompanying genealogy is even more tentative than those for the other drumships. Lotigo, the last head of the line, has died, and his wife Gudhul has produced only two pairs of girl twins. In 1949 she wished to be divorced and the family was very concerned about it. They felt that she had no right to a divorce, but said they had no objections to her living with whomsoever she chose, provided the children remained the legal heirs of Lotigo, and so, in due course, could assume the leadership of the family.

The Ngabilet clan which 'adopted' Dhorote has a special affinity with game in general, and with the white-eared cob in particular: they are spoken of as the 'game people'. Tradition has it that game came out of the ground when one day the ancestor of the Ngabilet was digging a well and came upon a horn—he pulled it out of the ground and brought out the first white-eared cob, which was followed by its doe and all manner of other species. The hole was then closed up so that the animals had perforce to remain on earth. The clan are supposed to make two grass rings, one of which they place on the game path, and the other they put in the River Kengen, when the game migration is due, as an invitation: all species of game are said to 'hear' this invitation except the giraffe and buffalo.

6. *The Longarim*

There seems little doubt that the Longarim were originally the fourth and junior drumship: when they left the rest of the tribe and moved to the Boya hills, their place was taken by the Ngenvac. The Murle always say that the Ngandarec are a Longarim clan, and Dhorote, who brought the drum, came from the Ngandarec Murle on the River Omo in Ethiopia. Possessing a drum he would, therefore, have a legitimate claim to the place vacated by the Longarim. The bulk of the Longarim now live in the Boya hills, far to the south of Murleland and close to the Didinga mountains. They have been separated for several generations, although the details of the quarrel which led to the separation are remembered.[1] In Lotilla there are three clans, Arec, Maindarec, and Ngandarec, said to be Longarim, but all claimed by the Ngarotti nowadays. It is, perhaps, significant that *arec* is the colour—large red spots on a white ground—applied to the giraffe, for shields are made of giraffe and buffalo hide, and the Longarim drum was the drum of

[1] Cf. p. 18.

the left hand, or shield arm. The main claim to fame of the
Longarim in Lotilla now is their ownership of the great shrines in
the river at Nyandit[1] and Abei. In their clan song they claim to be
the 'children of Nyallalec', which could mean of 'the wife of the
one who rubs the cow's head and back'. *Allal* is one of the
special terms of the cattle cult and refers to part of the ceremony
of *toven*.[2] The song includes the following lines:

> Our mother is as male, our mother is like a man;
> Our father used to drink honey,
> Keboh with his shield brought a drum home to the village.

This at least suggests that the Longarim were once the chief's
mother's people, and so correspond with the kinship category of
Ngoanidhet, and also that their drum was that of the left hand.
This suggestion may well be corroborated in a line of one of the
Tangajon songs which refers to the Longarim as the 'children of
their mother's sister', but it would need investigation with the
Longarim in the Boya hills.

From this investigation of the drumships it is clear that authority
is vested primarily in four families: the houses of Ngantin and
Lettec, a group which has taken the place of the Kelenya on the
Tangajon side of the country, and the Ngaicimut and Ngaloaga
families on the Ngarotti side. Members of the chiefly clan who are
not closely related to these families have little or no authority.
For this reason, chiefs who are always trying to attract followers
avoid doing anything without first consulting the elders, lest they
should be thought tyrannical or 'bitter', for a chief of this type
would tend to lose to other villages people not closely linked to
him.

7. *Mobility of Society*

This mobility of society is an essential part of their structure,
which acts as a safeguard against oppression by the chiefs, for there
are two reasons for belonging to a drumship—either residence in
its territory, or being born into one of the clans that traditionally
belong to the drumship in question. In the past the Murle clearly
regarded the latter criterion as the deciding factor, but at present,
when the great drumship ceremonies are falling into disuse, the

[1] Cf. p. 35.   [2] Cf. pp. 16, 32.

relative importance of the ties of residence, reinforced as they are by recent kinship links, is clearly greater, and is probably tending to become the more important factor. It is manifestly a cause of frequent disputes between chiefs, who try to claim the allegiance of every homestead residing in their villages, in spite of any previous loyalty to another chief. These movements of homesteads in themselves between villages and drumships are consistent with their contention that their clans have always been dispersed, and the dispersal of the Bulanec is another essential factor in the structure of society: it enables the framework of this clan to impose itself upon the tribe, so that when the unity of the Bulanec is stressed in opposition to the commoner-clans, it also underlines the unity of the whole tribe, a fact which is demonstrated at some of their ceremonies. Close relatives alone share in the inheritance of these families: they separate and represent the drum in different villages or groups of villages, and become members of those communities, seeking to cement their position by marrying their daughters to the clans living there. In the limited sphere of village activities they represent the drum in two senses: they act as chiefs, much as does the drumchief in the wider sphere of the whole drumship, because they act as his representative, and at the same time they become identified with the village, in turn linking it to the wider organization of the drumship through their membership of the ruling family. As was seen in the discussion of the previous chapter, the fact that all clansmen do not live in the area of their drumship is of little concern: the individual remains a member of his clan by birth, wherever he lives. The ties linking clansmen are weak, because the point of contact is remote compared with those formed by existing or remembered marriages in the recent past.

A commoner living in a village with which his clan is strongly associated, and within his drumship, does enjoy a slightly higher status than an outsider, but there is no compulsion on him to live in this village. From all the Murle say, this appears to have been just as true in the past, and certainly was the case in 1914, when Colonel Logan wrote that 'Villages are formed by the common agreement of the people who live there. The families are not necessarily under one chief and there is no compulsion to remain in the village.'[1]

[1] M. H. Logan, 'Manners and Customs of the Beirs', *Sudan Notes and Records*, vol. i, 1918.

The gradual elimination of the Kelenya and Ngenvac is part of the process of change: they have been replaced, for all practical purposes, by the house of Lettec and the lineage of Ngaloaga, and in a few generations the pattern of four drumships in opposed pairs will doubtless have been re-formed. It is only in the light of these considerations that their explanation of their tribal structure in terms of clans and drumships is valid. The courts recently set up by the Sudan Government are based on geographical convenience rather than historical ties, so that a further emphasis on the ties of residence has now been introduced. The Northern Court at Likwangoli, under the presidency of Lual, of the junior Tangajon, also includes the Tangon chiefship of Yankon, the Kelenya chiefship of Madhi Maraka, and the Ngarotti chiefships of Ibun Leberac, Lom Cankac, and Moa Oleo. The Central Court at Pibor Post, under the presidency of the Tangajon drumchief Korok Adeng, includes the Tangajon chiefships of Gogol, Ngandhelu, Kongkong Ibun, Lotilem, Dhrangira, and Guloc, and also the Ngarotti chiefship of Nganun Gola. The Southern Court at Ferteit, under the presidency of Kutek Ngatumo, acting drumchief of the Ngaicimut, also includes the Ngaicimut chiefship of Kengen Longoli, together with the Tangajon of Maruwa, under Keli Loden, and the Ngenvac of Korok Kavula; and, lastly, the Western Court at Gummuruk comprises the remaining Ngaloaga chiefs, under the presidency of Poti Burnian, acting drumchief of the Ngaloaga.

The relative importance of these chiefships is shown by the table opposite, compiled from the 1950 census.

MURLE CENSUS, 1950

	Total	Tangajon	Kelenya	Ngaroti	Ngenvac
Tangajon					
Korok Adeng	60	50	..	10	..
Gogol	38	18	1	17	2
Kongkong	70	38	..	26	6
Guloc	47	26	..	21	..
Lual	75	74	1	..	..
Yankon	65	61	2	2	..
Keli	44	8	2	34	..
Lotilem	40	18	..	22	..
	439	293	6	132	8
Kelenya					
Madhi Maraka	90	64	22	2	2
Ngarotti (Ngaloaga)					
Lom	39	..	1	38	..
Poti	120	3	10	98	9
Dhelu	103	11	4	59	29
Todoc	75	17	4	54	..
Allan	34	8	..	26	..
Ngatiligo	68	4	2	53	9
Logidang	98	5	4	88	1
Nyatu	61	..	..	61	..
	598	48	25	477	48
Nagarotti (Ngaicimut)					
Kutek	65	19	6	28	12
Kengen	69	..	..	69	..
Ibun Labarac	60	5	2	53	..
Nganun	116	44	6	58	8
	310	68	14	208	20
Ngenvac					
Korok Kavula	65	8	3	46	8
Total	1,502	481	70	865	86

IV

THE SACRED DRUMS AND THE
FUNCTIONS OF THE DRUMCHIEFS

ONE afternoon towards the end of March 1949, when I was sitting on the river bank at Likwangoli, a young member of the Tangajon chiefly line came to join the group of Murle with whom I was discussing their political system. After listening for a while the young man joined in the conversation, and his remarks implied that the chiefly system, the age-set system, and the kinship system were as 'hard' (or difficult, or important) as water and fire amongst the Murle, '*aladhet buldhet ke ben atendhet adoi ki maam ke ben guh Murle*', and then he added as an afterthought 'and wealth is nearly as important'. When the ceremonial significance of fire and water to them is remembered, the translation could mean: 'The chiefly system, the age-set system, and the kinship system are as fundamental to the Murle as the elements of fire and water (without which man cannot live).'

I was delighted, because this remark summed up in a characteristically Murle manner my own conclusions as to the way in which they themselves regard their own political institutions. I have taken it as the basis of this account, contrasting their explanation in terms of these three systems with my own observations of their territorial distribution and the structure of their villages.

The outstanding feature of the political system is the position of the drumchiefs at the head of the four drumships: by virtue of their guardianship of the sacred drums their spiritual powers are paramount, and although the exercise of these powers is hedged around by precedent, and the fear of incurring disaster should their ancestors be annoyed by the misuse of these powers, their formal pronouncements are treated with the greatest respect. Nobody would dream of approaching the drum without taking the appropriate ceremonial precautions, or of lightly incurring the drumchief's anger. The drums are at once symbols of tribal unity and of supernatural powers; they are the means whereby divine aid is invoked in time of war, when the rains fail, or when tribal unity is threatened by the refusal of one member to accept the considered verdict of chiefs and elders in council over a legal dispute. They also provide sanctuary for a killer from the revenge of the dead man's feud kin, and thus serve to prevent the dissipation of the tribe's manpower in internecine fighting.

Although the chiefly and age-set systems in combination provide most of the distinctive features of the political organization, a knowledge of the kinship system is essential for an understanding of Murle society, and of how the chiefly system works. They always explain their social structure in terms of drumships, clans, lineages, homesteads, and households, and it is in this respect another example of the predominantly patrilineal and patrilocal segmentary lineage systems to be found in so many African tribes. A group of households combine to form a homestead; a group of these form a *tatok* or minimal lineage, a group of *tatok* form a lineage, *bor*, a clan, *bang*, is formed of a group of lineages, and each drumship consists of a branch of the chiefly Bulanec clan and its attached commoner-clans. The drumships work in pairs to form sides, *ribir*; and the two sides, when they combine against a common foe, represent the whole tribe. Their political structure, as they explain it in terms of clans and drumships, might be expressed in the following diagram:

West side		East side	
Chiefs: Bulanec clan			
Ngenvac	Ngarotti	Tangajon	Kelenya
Commoner-Clans			
Ngabilet	Mainguli	Vorket	Riaka
	Golli	Vorom	Maintang
	Tangkok	Olginyon	Martok
	Ibbo	Kaijat	Tenu
		Ngaatibonga	Dhure
	Nganloki	Nayagudhul	Kanibor
	Anyang	Ngandoi	Agoi
	Arec	Dhooten	Maintamma
	Mainlokidang	Lotorongong	Girocol
	Mainlollo	Jimma	etc.
	Agoi and the	etc.	
	Lokicar		
	Teenad		
	Longarim		
	Ngandarec		
	Maindarec		
	etc.		

The drumchiefs are called *alaan ci kidongu*—literally 'chief of the drum'—and their close relatives are entitled to wear the *kondec*, the scarlet breast feathers of the Abyssinian *bobolink*, a bird belonging to the shrike family, on their heads. The heir of the drumchief wears this badge, to which Golmer refers in his song,[1] in the centre of his forehead; other relatives wear it a little to one side, and the more distant the relationship the further round the side of the head it is worn: thus they are referred to as 'chiefs of the shrike', *alaat ci kondecu.*

The drumchiefs derive their political authority from their religious influence as guardians of the sacred drums which they have inherited from their fathers under the rule of primogeniture. Some account of Murle religion must therefore be given if the position of these chiefs in the tribe is to be understood. Unfortunately, this is seldom formulated with any clarity: it is often necessary to study the rite or ceremony appropriate to a particular occasion or event to discover the underlying belief. The theory that a clan or lineage consists of the ancestors, the living, and those still to be born, is fundamental. The obligation to beget heirs to preserve this continuity governs many of their actions, and explains much of their attitude to the object of man's existence on earth. It also underlies many of the reciprocal obligations of the kinship system. A man's personal religion is, therefore, much concerned with the propitiation of his ancestors, and God is invoked only indirectly through them.

It is to their ancestral spirits that most Murle prayers are addressed, because their sense of continuity between the past, present, and future members of the tribe, and more particularly the clan, is so strong. It is this which explains why they want children so desperately (to carry on their line), and why they regard cattle as owned by the family. It is, therefore, to their ancestors who have passed on, but whom they feel are still interested, that they appeal for help and intervention with Tammu on all important occasions. In times of trouble, or when a misfortune occurs to an individual, they resign themselves to the will of God, *dodh ci Tammu*, and in the greatest tragedy of all, when the rains fail, it is to Tammu Kujen, rain (or God) which comes from the east, that whole communities pray at the rain dances, *turu*. It is, therefore, true to say that, so far as an individual or family is concerned, their

[1] Cf. p. 56.

religion contains a considerable element of ancestor-worship or intercession; but where the whole tribe is concerned, God is approached more directly through the drums, and at these ceremonies the drumchiefs have special ritual functions to perform.

1. *The Functions of the Drum*

The drums are regarded with the utmost awe: it is thought that if any unauthorized person were to touch one of them his skin would peel off and he would die. Instances of this having happened are quoted. Falling stars are believed to be on their way to the drums; women present beads to them in the hope of begetting children, and it is said that if a hut in which a drum is kept catches fire, it will roll out of its own accord. Although I was told of this happening to the junior Tangajon drum at Likwangoli, the Beir Patrol succeeded in burning the senior Tangajon drum in 1912, when they fired the hut in which it was kept.

The profound respect accorded to the drumchiefs derives naturally from their guardianship of the drums: indeed, when talking with the Murle, it is often difficult to know whether they refer to a chief or a drum, so great is the identification between the two. When Korok Adeng showed me his drum he first tied a piece of *lamurwa* round my wrist to ward off ill effects, and spat on my hands. Although he took the same precautions with my companion, Kortulia, a Government interpreter who might have been more sophisticated, the latter was patently terrified. Korok's drum was kept rolled up in a red blanket in the hut of his senior wife. It is said that leopard skins are often used for this purpose. The drum was about eighteen inches high and a foot across the top, tapering downwards to the base. Numerous thongs tied on the skin were festooned with blue earrings, which had been presented to the drum by women, in the hopes that each donor would be rewarded with a child. The drums are so sacred that they are very seldom used, and then only in real emergencies. The Murle feel that God and the departed chiefs would be annoyed if they were put to frivolous use, and they are, in fact, employed only in the following circumstances:

   (i) to invoke divine assistance in time of war;
  (ii) to bring rain in time of drought;
 (iii) to provide sanctuary in time of feud;

(iv) to outlaw a Murle who refuses to accept the decision of the assembled chiefs and elders in a case, or, as we should say, to provide the ultimate legal sanction;

(v) to invoke divine assistance for hunting.[1]

We may consider the first two of these.

(i) *In Time of War*

They are always most emphatic that the drum's part in war was its most important function. After a campaign had been decided upon, and the leaders selected, the warriors in full battle array used to go to the drumchief to secure his blessing. They made as if to charge his hut, and after a time the chief came out and everyone fled and lay down, for it was thought that if a warrior did not take cover quickly the drum would kill him for his presumption. After the greeting of the drum, *dhowinet ci kidongu*, had been repeated several times, the chief blessed the warriors by sprinkling them with ashes, *avac mura*; he then took his sacred spear and begged God to bless the enterprise and to make the warriors brave. He shook his spear in the enemy's direction, exhorting his warriors 'Let your spears be sharp! Capture many cattle! Drive the enemy away and scatter them!' Before returning the spear to its sheath he cleansed it symbolically with grass, as if wiping off the blood of the foe. The warriors set off after this ceremony, accompanied by a specially selected man, belonging to the clan, with the hereditary duty of carrying the sacred firesticks: to him the chief gave some of his own firesticks, from which all fires on the march were lighted.

If the attack proved successful, all the captured cattle were driven back to the drumchief's homestead. A great dance of the drum was held, at which the cattle, save those captured by men of the Bulanec clan, were divided. Slaves captured in war were the property of their captors. The division, *ngerin*, was made, at least nominally, by the drumchief, who reserved a large share for the drum which had provided supernatural aid. Warriors who had fought well received the reward of their prowess, and no doubt the institution served a valuable purpose by ensuring that they concentrated on fighting rather than feathering their own nests.

This custom can only have provided a rough-and-ready form of

[1] Cf. p. 33.

justice, for it is frequently spoken of as having been very 'bitter', *kaaka*, and if the chief disliked a man for any reason he stood small chance of sharing in the spoils. In the past the dances of successful warriors, when the drum was beaten in triumph, were the greatest moments in Murle life, and today there is no substitute. Before returning home the warriors were ceremonially purified by the chief,[1] who scattered drops of water over them from his sacred gourd, to prevent the dangerous effects of shedding human blood from harming their kinsfolk; and, as a sign that he came in peace, every warrior who had shed blood had to wear a metal ring round his ankle or toe, and to pick a bunch of *lamurwa* and throw it on every homestead before greeting his relatives.

For a tribe which values cattle so highly, every year of whose history is remembered for some military success or disaster, whose whole life and social organization were geared to war, this particular function of the drumchief cannot be over-emphasized.

(ii) *Rainmaking*

Rainmaking was a vital function, because starvation followed drought. There would be no grazing for the cattle, no crops, and in the dry river beds no fish. This, however, seems to have taken second place to the military function of the drumchiefs, possibly because the rains did not often fail, and because of their primarily pastoral values. On Boma, with its incidence of tsetse fly, agriculture is the main source of livelihood, and rain, consequently, of greater relative importance. There the ritual functions of the owner of the land are more in evidence than in the villages of the Lotilla plains. In the Ngarotti lands nobody can remember when the rain dances were last held; on Boma there was one as recently as 1947, and I have talked with people who were present. In the great drought year of 1914 the Tangajon held dances night after night, the noise they made being referred to in early military reports from Pibor Post. In 1921 an important dance was held at the junction of the Lotilla and Kengen rivers, to celebrate the arrival of the drum captured by the Boma Murle from the Dhuak (Suri), and sent to Korok Adeng, as head of the family, to replace that lost by fire in 1912. Although I was told that rain songs were sung on this occasion, it seems probable that it was more a dance of thanksgiving.

[1] Cf. p. 78.

These variations may partly explain the relative importance ascribed to the rainmaking properties of the drum. Rainmaking is very largely a woman's affair, and on Boma, where, as has been noted, life depends on agriculture, rain is all-important. On the Veveno and Upper Lotilla the Ngarotti grow very little grain, because they possess large herds of cattle on which they live: some of their repeated raids on the Dinka of Bor District for cattle and slaves are within living memory, and their interest in their drum's magical properties is inevitably centred on war rather than rainmaking. In the central and northern area of the Kelenya and Tangajon drumships the economy is more mixed; if the rains are late, cattle can always be driven to the swamps, and grain plays a greater part in their economy.

The rain dance, *turo* (pl. *turin*), for which special songs were sung, was unlike the normal Murle dance, *kurma*. Men and women danced in long lines round and round the drum, which was beaten by the women. The lines of dancers moved in opposite directions, and during the dance a man could greet any woman he liked by throwing a little dry mud at her; the women were permitted to do the same to the men of their choice. This greeting was an invitation to sexual intercourse, and, if accepted, the pair would slip away to a convenient house or into the bush. No objections and no claims for adultery could be raised: if disapproval was expressed they would retort: 'Are we not praying to God for rain?' In the old days it is said that young men had no wish to marry a girl who did not know how to perform the rain dances properly.

On these occasions the women dressed like men, wearing skin chest-protectors, *bokor*, and carried sticks. The senior wife of the drumchief, *ngai ci kaka*, the 'wife of bitterness', of whom everybody was afraid, was the principal performer. Only fully initiated men who had killed their man in war were entitled to take part, and the older men, who were unable to dance for long, sat round watching, while the younger men kept their distance.

In some villages the local chief's wife took a pot, tied a skin over its mouth, and this was beaten instead of a drum, otherwise the procedure was similar. An ox or a sheep was sacrificed, and the wife of the chief took some of the intestinal grass, together with cattle dung, and threw it up into the air. On Boma the sacrifice was made at a special rock on which some of the intestinal grass was smeared by the wife of the chief. At the end of the dance those present were blessed by the chief, who sprinkled holy water over them.

The rain dances were the nearest approach to a religious festival to be found amongst the Murle. They were also fertility rites at which promiscuity was permissible to initiated men, and the fact that these dances persisted longer on Boma may be because initiation was continued there for three more age-sets than amongst the Lotilla Murle. I suspect, however, that the rain rock on Boma was sacred to the Suri before the Murle arrived, and that their greater dependence on agriculture was the compelling reason for still holding rain dances there.

There is a family on the Veveno which has rainmaking powers, *ol ci kirir*. When they wish to make rain they hang a gourd of water at the top of a tree, bathe in a pool, return to the tree, and cut down the gourd, so that it falls and breaks: rain is said to fall the same day. This family is descended from a man captured from the Dinka, and their special powers derive from the sacred spear of the Nyarraweng Dinka. It provides an interesting commentary on the troubled history of the borderlands between Nuer, Dinka, and Murle. The latter members of the family were captured by the Lau Nuer from the Dinka, and later taken into captivity from them by the Murle. Descendants of this family now live with all three, and although they are unable to speak each other's language, their relationship is still recognized.

It is claimed that in days gone by, when a chief wished to go on a journey during the dry weather, he would call for a half-gourd of water, dip in his sandals, and then wave them to the sky so that drops fell to the ground like rain. They believe that God heard his prayers and sent clouds to shade his journey. Some informants said that the drumchief used the same procedure at rain dances, although it was his wife's throwing cattle dung into the air that was considered more important. Nevertheless, the chief's blessing of the assembled people by sprinkling them with water from his own gourd was an essential part of the rite, as it still is in the settlement of disputes.

2. *Customary Law*

For a variety of reasons I found Murle law an intricate subject. Although a few legal principles are known to everybody, it consists chiefly of case law, and invoking precedents forms an essential part of the procedure. Further, there is a paucity of legal terms, *ker ci Murlu*,[1] which have to indicate anything from the law relating to a serious crime to an unimportant breach in accepted behaviour, such as might occur, for example, at a marriage ceremony and might 'annoy the ancestors' of the kinsfolk concerned. In addition, there is no theoretical distinction between civil and criminal law, although, as will be seen later, the beginnings of this concept do exist. The majority of important cases concern the complicated subject of inheritance, for which my records are incomplete. In consequence, I have attempted only an outline of their attitude to what we should call minimal law, treating the whole subject as customary law rather than drawing a distinction between the two. With their keen sense of straightness or justice, *leminet*, this may be less than fair to them, and it certainly limits the following account of their customary law to the particular field with which I was most concerned.

Before describing the hearing of a case the position of the spokesmen, *gayoi*, must be considered. I have used this word advisedly: *gayoi* is derived from the stem *aga* 'to know', for although most elders aspire to the distinction of being *gayoi*, only a few, and those with outstanding powers of eloquence, in fact acquired it. There was, indeed, a considerable element of heredity in the position; sons of fathers learned in the law tended to assimilate something of their fathers' knowledge and follow in their footsteps, while many elders were of too shy and retiring a disposition to achieve eminence in this field. *Gayoi* play an important part in the social life of the tribe, and those with histrionic abilities have an opportunity to display their talents to a large audience, as well as serving to remind the community of the details of the law, and so hand it on from one generation to another, thus preserving tribal tradition and providing a check on the abuse of power by the chiefs.

Disputes amongst the Murle are normally settled by the elders sitting in conclave at the village clubs. Only really important cases were referred to the drumchief for settlement, and, even then, were in effect tried by the elders; but behind the acceptability of their decisions lay the enforcement of their ruling by the drumchief, who would curse those refusing to abide by them. The ceremony of cursing with the drum, *atoo kidonga*, was comparatively simple: the drumchief took his drum and sacred spear to the homestead

[1] Cf. p. 19.

of the guilty party, accompanied by a group of his own relatives and the elders. There, to the accompaniment of the drum, which was beaten by an attendant, he cursed the offender and drew a line on the ground across the entrance to his homestead. Thereafter, under pain of supernatural death, no one could offer the culprit food or drink. I was told that on the few occasions when resort was had to this drastic action the offender almost invariably ran away and took refuge with a neighbouring tribe before the arrival of the drumchief.

3. *Settlement of Cases*

Those cases that were heard before a drumchief provided a long, drawn-out and impressive performance. Each was expected to last at least three days, and the proper time for giving judgement was the late afternoon. The elders sat in a group under a large shady tree, the chief and his relatives forming another group, while the children, women, and warriors kept a respectful distance. The elders appointed one of their number to 'receive' or 'echo' the statement of the complainant. The latter and his echo stood up probably at a distance of several paces, stating his case in a very slow, clear, and deliberate manner, in short sentences or phrases. Almost every word he said was repeated by the echo, particularly the last few words. Through the echo he was then questioned by the chiefs, and the defendant was asked to reply, which he did in a similar manner. Next, the complainant was requested to produce his witnesses, one of the elders standing up to take their evidence, and this was followed by the hearing of witnesses called for the defence.

Throughout the procedure the witness under examination was allowed to talk only to the elder deputed to receive his evidence; it was absolutely forbidden for the complainant to address the defendant directly or for witnesses of either side to address each other. If defendant or complainant was a young man, a woman, or a child, the case was opened by his representative, the head of the homestead, he or she, if necessary, being called as a witness later.

When all the evidence had been taken by the elders, anyone who had anything to contribute to the case rose and had his say, again speaking to someone deputed to receive his speech. Principles and precedents were invoked and similarities and differences between comparable cases in the past carefully considered. Eventually the elders came to their conclusion and turned to the chiefs, who until then had taken no active part in the proceedings, except, possibly, suggesting a question to be put to one of the witnesses. One of the elders 'explained' the case to the drumchief or one of his relatives. When they had elicited all the information they wished from the elders, they withdrew to consider the verdict. The chiefs, who all wore the *kondec* on their heads and had blackened their faces with charcoal or soot, returned when they had made their decision. They sat down deliberately and called a commoner over to them. They told him their finding, which he announced, sometimes after climbing the tree under which the chiefs were sitting, though this was done only when the announcer thought the finding might be unpopular, or when the loser belonged to a powerful clan. He announced the finding by shouting repeatedly: '*Alem giten, volong giten*', 'So-and-so is in the right, So-and-so is empty.'

All the assembled chiefs then rose, surrounded the winner, and walked round the meeting-place in a body, singing the song of judgement, *caal ci paiyinto*. This continued for some little time, the announcer meanwhile shouting out the names of various bygone chiefs: 'Gugu *apak*! Letec *apak*! Gugu gave judgement, Lettec gave judgement; they have gone but their sons remain. Listen Tangajon, listen Ngenvac, listen Ngarotti, listen Kelenya, Korok Adeng has given judgement, the chief of the Murle has given judgement, So-and-so is in the right, So-and-so is guilty.'

(When discussing this part of the proceedings with me, my informants laid considerable stress on the fact that Korok Adeng, the present drumchief of the Tangajon drumship, gives judgement by virtue of direct descent from his predecessors. All four drumships are symbolically told of the decision, because once the song of judgement has been sung the case is settled for all time in their eyes; there is no question of appeal: the case cannot be reopened, and if, as very occasionally happened in the past, the losing side objected, the drumchief enforced the sentence by threatening dissidents with the drum.)

After this interlude the chiefs returned to their places, one of their number standing up to work out the sentence with the co-operation of the elders. As in more advanced societies, the full judgement consisted of the finding and sentence. The latter almost always involved the payment of cattle, and although these may be classified into bulls and cows, heifers and oxen, they vary greatly in value. The Murle, being expert judges of cattle, haggle for hours over the payment of a customary due expressed in, for instance, the term 'four cows and two oxen'. In reaching a settlement particular cows have to be mentioned by their colour conformation; precedents about payments in similar circumstances in the past are quoted, and, if sufficient cattle cannot be produced or promised at the time, cattle have to be promised from the next marriage of a daughter of the loser's kin. Thus it is easy to appreciate that the working-out of a sentence was an involved part of the settlement. The loser naturally protested that he had no cattle, and this was hotly refuted by the winners, who suggested that they were hidden with kinsmen, and the elders were prompted to ask about a particular beast.

The strength of this procedure for the settlement of disputes lay in the fact that they were tried in public by a jury of elders who took a pride in their knowledge of the law and were concerned with their reputation for fair dealing. In addition, they presented their findings to the chief who, by virtue of his hereditary position as guardian of the drum, 'cut' (*apak*) the case, the supernatural sanction of outlawry providing a reinforcement to the decision.

The weakness of the system, on the other hand, lay in the fact that it was cumbersome and sometimes the complainant had no means of persuading the chief to set the procedure in motion. The criticism that a man with few relatives found it difficult in the past to get justice was all too often a fair one. Undoubtedly the chiefs sometimes placed obstacles in the way, especially if the case involved a rich man, one of their relatives, or a member of an important clan. Armed self-help, or the threat of it, played a considerable part in the legal system, and it was often necessary for a plaintiff to secure his kinsmen's help to get the machinery of conciliation set in motion before the chief. In consequence, it was a great handicap to be an orphan or to belong to a small lineage.

If fighting threatened, or broke out, the relatives-in-law of both sides, and neighbouring elders, hastened to intervene, and public opinion was often sufficiently strong to ensure that the dispute was settled in the customary manner. As with so many things in Murle society, practice fell far short of theory, however admirable, and the best insurance a man could have that his rights would be protected was to have the support of a numerous lineage or to be well connected by marriage, in order to count on the assistance which these relatives were obliged to give under the kinship system.

In most instances, however, so traditional is their love of order and correct behaviour, coupled with great respect for age and the rulings of the elders, that public opinion in a village generally does ensure the acceptance of a reasonable settlement, and it is only when the ordinary procedure of conciliation has broken down, and one of the families concerned is guilty of some further provocation, that reference to the chiefs and the invocation of a formal case before the drumship court is necessary. Indeed, commoners often laugh at the chiefs because they are unable to settle their own family quarrels: the difficulty, of course, is that the elders, who speak their minds fearlessly in a dispute amongst commoners, are nervous of intervening between powerful chiefs.

4. *Case Summaries*

The following summaries serve to illustrate some of the points of Murle law. They were all reported to me when I was District Commissioner of the Murle, and are very brief accounts of complicated events.

(i) At Ferteit on the Kengen river in 1937 Golmathi Nganma's younger brother stole a sheep, killed it, and was cooking it, when the owner came up and seized him by the arm, saying: 'That is my sheep.' The thief, fearing that the story would get about and everybody laugh at him for a thief, stabbed the owner in the belly and ran away. Later the relatives of the deceased found the body, and a stick which they recognized as belonging to the thief. They went to Golmathi's homestead and accused the thief of having killed the owner of the sheep, which at first he denied. They then brought some butter fat and asked him to eat it with the relatives of the deceased. He refused. This was accepted as conclusive evidence of his guilt.

The relatives of the deceased summoned their kinsmen and, armed with sticks, went to Golmathi. They said to him: 'Your brother has killed our brother.' He replied: 'Yes it is a bad business, go and beat him and kill him.' The murderer and thief had gone hunting; the deceased's kinsmen followed him and beat him to death, throwing their sticks on top of the corpse. The murderer's relatives held no burial ceremony for him.

(ii) A wizard named Madhi Aleikonu killed a man called Kelang at

Boma in 1936. Kelang's clan, the Olginyon, went to the head of the Maijath clan and said that they wanted to kill Madhi because he was a wizard and had killed Kelang. The Maijath admitted that Madhi was indeed a wizard, and claimed no compensation when the Olginyon beat the murderer to death with sticks.

(iii) Oleo was a wizard living at Toddo, the southern-most village of the Lotilla. He was believed to have killed a number of people and cattle by witchcraft. In 1932 a whispering campaign started against him; he had been caught several times and ransomed himself with a bracelet, hoes, or something of the sort. The people banded together and went to the local chief. The community decided that he must pay the death penalty; the chief endorsed their decision, and one evening all the young men went to his village after dark, found Oleo sitting down by the fire, and beat him to death with sticks.

(iv) In 1932 a man on Boma, named Abutha Ibun, wished to have sexual intercourse with a woman called Ngarreko, wife of Agirgir Rio. She always refused. One day when she was hoeing her grain plot he went to her, said that he had killed an animal in some near-by bush, and told her to come and collect some of the meat. This conversation was over-heard by her small son. She went with Abutha into the bush, where he stabbed her to death, because she refused to satisfy his demands. Her relatives at length found her body and started to make inquiries. Her small boy repeated the conversation he had overheard between his mother and Abutha. Her relatives then charged Abutha with her murder. He denied the story, but that night ran to the chief's house for sanctuary. A few days later the murdered woman's clansmen went to the chief, who handed him over, and he was beaten to death; no compensation was claimed by his relatives.

(v) In 1940 a young man named Kowan Baatingantong was hanged by his elder brother and mother on the path at Gicinyero for being a confirmed thief. He had been imprisoned in 1939 by the chiefs and Captain Alban for stealing goods from the merchant's shop at Vorcileimen. This did not cure him, however, and he continued to steal; his relatives were being threatened frequently by people claiming compensation for his thefts. Eventually his mother and brother could stand it no longer, and about six months after his release from prison, hanged him from a tree.

(vi) In 1938 a man named Keili Baatingatil killed his wife's lover with a stick. His kinsmen did not support him strongly, saying that they were not too sure about the adultery. He accordingly ran away to the Adonga Anuak, where he eventually managed to buy a child from the Anuak, which they had stolen from the Masango in Anyssinia. This child he paid in compensation and then returned to his village.

5. *Justifiable Homicide*

The Murle consider that in certain circumstances an individual is justified in taking a wrongdoer's life: these are:

(i) if he catches a witch or wizard in the act of performing his evil practices;[1]

(ii) if he catches another man in the act of committing adultery with his wife;[2]

(iii) if he catches a man in the act of stealing his property.[3] Normally a man is not expected to go to such lengths; he is entitled to beat the offender but not, as a rule, so violently as to cause death. In no circumstances is he allowed to use a spear or any other weapon made of steel.

There are two reasons underlying this part of the law. First, it is recognized that the wronged man may have to fight with the wrongdoer; the law gives him a measure of protection because it realizes he is free to defend himself so violently as to cause the death of the offender in the process. It is, therefore, in a sense, an extension of the right of self-defence. Second, this right is granted to individuals only when the wrongdoer has committed an offence which is regarded as an anti-social act as well as a private wrong against the individual concerned.

The fear of the evil effects of shedding human blood is very profound amongst the Murle; even in the socially approved action of killing an enemy purification is essential before normal life may be resumed.[4] Even when these precautions have been taken, the killer is not considered completely normal until the attendant birds[5] or spirits of the dead man have been exorcized by a doctor at a special ceremony. This procedure differs little from the rites performed after natural death.

6. *Feud and the Hurt Ceremony*[6]

Although intentional homicide is extremely rare, unintentional homicide does occur fairly frequently; most commonly it is through hunting accidents, occasionally from injuries received when fishing, and sometimes from wounds received in stick fights. In all these circumstances a state of feud comes into force between the kin of the deceased and that of the killer, whether or not

[1] Cf. p. 143.   [2] Cf. p. 123.   [3] Cf. p. 145.
[4] Cf. p. 69.   [5] Cf. pp. 128, 136.   [6] Cf. p. 107.

compensation, *ngabolo*, is payable. Compensation is payable for death as a result of a hunting accident, but not for death caused by a fish-hook wound: this is due to a judgement by a Murle chief in the past which is always quoted as a precedent—the elders say: 'He was stabbed by a particular kind of fish, not by a human being', *akat ngenge lang akat et ci deer*. Whatever the details of the case which produced this ruling, or the general considerations which influenced the particular chief, the precedent has persisted and become law. Possibly it may have been held that it was everyone's duty in such a communal activity, when spears and fish-hooks are always being thrust under water, to look out for himself. In any case, fatal accidents of this nature appear to be rare. A similar formula is invoked in fatal hunting accidents: the chiefs say: 'He wanted meat, he did not want to kill a man'; this traditional formula clearly gives a lead to settlement of the feud by payment of the compensation awarded for deaths caused by stick wounds, and its application depends on the particular circumstances of each case, above all on whether or not the giver of the fatal blow has performed the *mayuwanet* or 'hurt ceremony'.

Feud amongst the Murle is very different from the comparable institution with the Nuer, where the leopard-skin chief provides a method of mediation only if both parties so desire. Even if a settlement has been effected by the ceremonial transfer of blood-wealth in the form of cattle, a state of tension remains between the two lineages concerned, which may easily break out again into fighting, with resulting deaths. With the Nuer it is, more than any other factor, the degree of relationship between the lineages concerned that decides whether or not a feud is settled. A Nuer's kin stand by him and the dispute is settled by negotiation, or further fighting between the lineages. Amongst the Murle, on the other hand, the feud is settled by the drumchief to whom the killer flies for sanctuary. The chief announces to the tribe that he has given sanctuary to the killer, and if he finds any of the dead man's feud kin skulking round his *korok*, trying to take revenge, he prevents them; he tells them: 'Let the dead man rest, the killer will find something for you.' He may even curse them for 'wanting to shed blood' in his *korok*.

The importance of the chiefly system is again apparent when the 'slave' is handed over in compensation: the killer's kin hand him over to the chief, who appoints a day for handing him over to the kin of the dead man, when they come to take the boy; the chief and his family keep the two groups apart. An old chief described the procedure as follows:

He takes them to the river; the people bathe. When the dead man's people approach, the killer's people stand up: they run away leaving the 'slave boy'. The dead man's people take their property, the 'slave boy', in place of their own boy. The chief, with whom the killer took sanctuary, goes on to the path before the killer's kinsmen leave. He takes some '*dumari*' sticks and puts them on a fire; the killer stands in the smoke of this fire; the chief waves the smoke against his body, saying: 'Let this smoke take away the old story, let him be good, let no harm befall him.' At the end the killer is told to 'go in peace'.

As a result, feuds were rare and, if they occurred, did not assume the political importance they had amongst the Nuer. In 1943 I became personally involved in a case of feud: a certain Ngaicaluk killed a fellow tribesman with a spear and neglected to perform the customary *mayuwanet* ceremony, although he had plenty of time to do so. The Murle were outraged, Ngaicaluk was arrested and brought to me at Likwangoli, and, in the eyes of everyone present, was guilty of murder. With a heavy heart I held a magisterial inquiry, knowing that if proved guilty he could only be charged, under the Sudan Penal Code, with homicide (killing with a spear in free fight not being considered murder in the eyes of the Government), the maximum sentence for which was a long term of imprisonment.

Having heard and recorded the evidence, keenly watched by a large gathering of chiefs and elders, I announced that the prisoner would have to stand his trial for murder—or culpable homicide. My audience not understanding the legal distinction, or realizing that cases of murder were normally tried by a Major Court, started to sing the songs of judgement, for in their eyes he was proved guilty and the appropriate penalty was death. I checked the singing and explained that under Government law such an important case could not be tried by one man, but had to be brought before a special court, and until this was done Ngaicaluk would remain in custody. How far they understood is open to question, for although they disapproved of the trial of such a case by one man, the court before them, consisting of numerous chiefs and elders under my presidency, constituted a sufficiently impressive court to try any case.

Continuing my journey to Pibor Post, I left the handcuffed prisoner behind, in charge of police, to follow on foot. On the way he attempted to escape and was shot dead by the police escort. The Murle considered this to be the judgement of God, and were delighted that justice had been done, while I was relieved of the impossible task of explaining to the Chief Justice in Khartoum that the prisoner was guilty of murder in the eyes of his tribesmen, for which the only appropriate punishment was death.

This illustrates the difficulty of reconciling customary law with the law of the land, as expressed in the Sudan Penal and Criminal Procedure Codes. Had Ngaicaluk been condemned to a period of imprisonment—the inevitable outcome of sending his trial papers to Khartoum—my authority and that of the chiefs and chief-police would inevitably have been undermined, and tribal discipline would have suffered. This case illustrates the advantage that a District Commissioner who has won the confidence of his people possesses in acquiring information about tribal law. The case was a *cause celèbre*, discussed that year wherever I went, the old men vying with each other in evoking comparable cases from the recesses of their memories, and incidentally teaching me a great deal about *ruwen dilawa*, murder by spearing.

What damned Ngaicaluk's behaviour so effectively in their eyes was the fact that he had failed to perform *mayuwanet* after wounding his victim, in the interval of a few days before the latter's death; nor did his attitude at the magisterial inquiry help him in this respect, for he protested that he would do it again and again, and showed no signs of repentance.

7. *The Death of a Chief*

Great distinction is made between the death of a commoner and that of a chief. The former concerns only his own immediate relatives and friends; the latter is a tragedy affecting the whole tribe, or at least the drumship concerned. The one is a social event, the other political: both require the appropriate ceremonies, and, although the chief's family have to perform the same ceremonies of purification as do those of a commoner's family, there is in addition the tribal or drumship ceremony of burial to be performed by all the warriors of the drumship. Unlike commoners, chiefs are buried, and cairns are built over their graves, to which every warrior should contribute a stone.

Because of the public nature of a chief's burial the corpse is not usually buried at once, but put on a platform in the hut in which he died. The hut is then carefully sealed up and surrounded with thorns, the *korok* being deserted except for a few old people left to guard it from harm. When the time for burial comes the drum is beaten and everyone assembles. The procession is headed by the senior wife, carrying her husband's remains on her head, and although she probably receives help during the journey, it is her ritual duty to perform this last service for her dead husband. Behind her comes the drum, carried by a close relative, and sounded mournfully from time to time. This is followed by a slave captured in war driving captured cattle; there follow the drumchief's family and relatives, and all the old warriors assembled to pay their last respects to their dead leader.

The cortège does not move fast or far in one day; at every stopping-place one of the oxen is killed to provide food for the party. Eventually the chosen burial-place is reached, where the site of the grave is selected and dug by the warriors, who are assisted by everyone present; from time to time the slave is made to lie down in it to see if the grave is large enough. Eventually the slave is told to slaughter an ox over the grave so that it is well drenched with blood. I was never able to discover what happened to the slave, except that he died. One informant told me that after eating meat of the slaughtered ox he was put into the grave alive, the chief's remains and the rest of the meat being put on top of him, and the grave then being filled in by the warriors, who piled stones on top of it to form a cairn. As this informant said: 'In the old days chiefs were very harsh!' No other informants would corroborate this: some said that the slave died from the effects of eating the chief's meat, as this drove him mad; others suggested that he was forcibly fed until he could eat no more and died of overeating. In any case, the question is only of academic interest, because no drumchiefs have been buried with full honours for many years past, since the necessary slaves and captured cattle no longer exist. However the slave died, it is abundantly clear that the chief was in some way provided with a servant to look after his needs in the underworld, and with food to sustain him on his journey.

Traditionally the Tangajon chiefs were buried at Mount Inidh in the Maruwa hills, and the Ngarotti chiefs at Mount Ngaronggoda to the south-west. Korok Adeng's immediate ancestors were buried near the river bank at Tangajon village, near Pibor Post, and Gugu, perhaps the most famous of all the old Tangajon chiefs, was buried with his sister at Kather (Mount Kathiangor) to the south of Maruwa.

In the case of chiefs closely related to the drumchief a modified ceremony was held. Their bodies were carried out to the east of the village, as opposed to those of commoners, which were exposed to the west. No grave was dug, but a cairn of sticks, stones, and earth was built over their remains, and today whenever a Murle passes one of these he is supposed to add a stick or stone and remove his sandals as a mark of respect. It is thought that if anybody should chance to sleep near one of these graves by mistake, a shower of rain would fall, irrespective of the time of year, and a number of cases of this having happened were quoted to me.

It is clear that the Murle turn to God and try to invoke his assistance through the medium of the drum in all major crises which affect the tribe. A distinction is made, however, between the values of God and of the drum. Warriors turn to it for help before going to war, and for purification on their return; middle-aged men, and women in particular, look to the drum: the former for rain in time of drought and the latter for children when they are barren; the elders and chiefs rely on the drum as a sanction for their judgements. God,[1] on the other hand, is generally regarded as remote and indifferent to individuals. In family and personal matters, therefore, the head of the homestead, with his sacred firesticks, acts as an intermediary in invoking the aid of the spirits of the ancestors, who are felt to be concerned with the doings of their descendants and more able to approach God. It is only in the provision of sanctuary for a killer that the drum's help is invoked by an individual, and in this case the drum acts as a symbol of tribal unity, by preventing the death of more members of the tribe.

[1] Cf. p. 127.

V

THE AGE-SET SYSTEM

'THE business of the age-sets is a weighty matter', *dodh ci-bulu dodh c'adingding*. Cutting right across all other distinctions, although mainly social today, the age-sets were primarily military in the past, and stratified the manpower of the tribe into divisions with their own distinctive colours, songs, and names. Each age-set is allotted a task suitable to the age and standing of its members, who, as they grow older, gradually progress through the grades of warriorhood, junior elderhood, and finally full elderhood, the highest grade of all. It is the members of the last grade who hear cases and decide on tribal policy, under the presidency of the chiefs; the junior elders raise families, provide the reserve of warriors in times of trouble, and cultivate crops; while the warriors form a standing guard for the protection of the country, and have the duty of herding the cattle. The underlying reason for the system was military necessity: since they were living at enmity with all their neighbours, the main function of their political organization, which consisted of the chiefly and age-set systems, was military—the whole tribe was geared for defence or attack.

That they were great fighters in the past is clear, not only from the fear they still inspire in the Dinka, and the respect given them by the Anuak (who latterly turned the tables on them, as they did on the Nuer, through their possession of firearms obtained from Abyssinia), but also from the early military reports of Bimbashi Comyn,[1] Captain Kelly,[2] Bimbashi Hutton,[3] and others. These

[1] *Monthly Intelligence Reports*; cf. pp. 6–8.

[2] 'That they possess the military spirit strongly is shown not only by their raids on the Dinka, but by their methods during the present expedition; their system of scouting, and the method of covering their tracks were excellent, whilst their bravery was beyond dispute' (Captain Wellby in his report on the Beir Patrol 1912, *Monthly Intelligence Report*, 1913).

[3] 'The Beirs fight at night, at daylight they will retire, but will attack again at sundown, creeping through the grass with their bodies smeared with mud. They always strike at the enemy's line of retreat' (M. H. Logan, 'Manners and Customs of the Beirs'). Logan's work was first published in *M.I.R.* and subsequently in *Sudan Notes and Records*, vol. i (1918); it was largely compiled from notes by the late Major Hutton and others.

comments accord with what the Murle say of their methods. When attacked they scattered, each man driving off his own cattle as best he could, leaving scouts to report on the progress of the enemy. The tribe would then muster and strive to cut off the raiding party as it withdrew: undoubtedly they were often successful, and ambushed a number of Nuer raiding parties during the hours of darkness.

Although the old men complain today that it was the imposition of the *Pax Britannica* which put an end to the military system, it is significant that initiation, *tedjandhet*, an institution formerly of prime importance, ceased some ten or twenty years before 1912. The reason given is *Mainlorien*, 'a monster the size of a small mountain', which stalked the country one year, killing all the cattle and eventually disappearing in Bolitingano Pool on the Kengen. Whatever the truth of this, it is certain that some epidemic killed off the cattle, and so effectively suspended initiation ceremonies which involved the sacrifice of considerable numbers of oxen: as far as I could establish *Mainlorien* appears to have occurred around 1890.[1] Amongst the cattle-less Boma Murle, however, initiation persisted for three more age-sets. As a result almost every plains Murle today is still a 'baboon', *ngane lotima*, an uninitiate.

Since 1912 the position has changed considerably. The military organization is decaying, together with much of the old political system; the drumchiefs are no longer independent, but subject to a District Commissioner and his police. In trying to understand how this very important factor in their political structure works today, however, it is necessary to explore its function in the past.

1. *Initiation*

The initiation ceremony itself, important *rite de passage* that it was, does not seem to have been such a painful ordeal as in some other tribes. Youths who felt the time had come for their initiation would behave provocatively to their seniors, who were frequently reluctant to be relegated to the position of village men, and sometimes posted guards on the drumchief's *korok* to prevent any approach to him. The old men contend that because of this reluctance, and the fact that the defence of the tribe depended on the warriors, the age at which a set entered the warrior grade was later

[1] Cf. pp. 154, 156.

then than today. Now it is the girls who really decide the matter when they say the senior warrior age-set is 'too old for flirting and wants women', it is time for them to give place to a younger set.

Although I made repeated attempts to obtain an account of the ceremony from the few initiates still living, they were too old or forgetful to remember much of the procedure of initiation. It is said to have been performed by the captains of previous sets, *nyakangen*, for whom it was thought to be extremely dangerous The initiates spent some days in the bush being taught tribal lore and the rules of behaviour, after which each had to produce a bull, which was speared, although sometimes two or more lads shared a bull which they 'killed together, all holding on to the spear at the same time'.[1] The entrails were then examined by the old men, who might declare the omens unpropitious, in which event another bull would have to be produced on a later day. Having killed their bull, the initiates had to carry handfuls of the intestinal grass clasped to their stomachs between the lines of old warriors, who thrashed them across their shoulders and backs with withies. On no account must they cry out or flinch, and if any of them dropped any of the grass he incurred lifelong scorn. Special songs were sung at these ceremonies, which were attended by the young men of a whole district.

Although the age-set system has persisted, the abandonment of initiation has undoubtedly produced a marked change in society. Many of the old ceremonies were reserved for the initiated warrior who had killed his man in war, for this condition had to be fulfilled before a young man attained full warriorhood and could participate in the war dances of the drum. Adopted Murle, although accepted as members of their captors' families for all practical purposes, were debarred from taking part in certain ceremonies because they were not 'true Murle', *Murle dedde*.

Immediately a set was initiated it started agitating, urging the elders to plan a campaign, *koodh*, against one of the neighbouring tribes, so that the new warriors could blood their spears in battle without delay. Campaigns were planned during the heavy rains and usually carried out at the end of that season, when sufficient

[1] Dr. Peristiany, who has seen initiation ceremonies amongst the Kipsigis and Suk, tells me that it is not the actual killing of the ox, which is done by all the initiates holding on to the spear together, but the ceremonial cutting-up of the meat afterwards. This is probably the explanation of the Murle version given above.

water remained in the pools to allow the warriors to cross the uninhabited spaces between the tribes; or during the early rains when similar conditions prevailed. In theory a campaign was organized and directed by one of the drumchiefs, but in practice it was the elders who made the decision, and the actual control of the fighters was entrusted to an old *nyakangen* appointed for the battle. Success in war was their greatest attainment, and for an old *nyakangen* to be chosen for this duty—later named after him —was a signal honour, particularly if his plan proved successful. There are very few men alive who have qualified for the proud title of *toromec*, great warrior, applied to a man who had killed an enemy while defending his own *korok*, as this was held to denote far greater courage than was required to kill an enemy in his own territory when the advantage of surprise lay with the attacker. Today, if a young man is seeking fame, he goes hunting, and the killer of a dangerous animal, *kelek ci moti*, such as lion, leopard, buffalo, elephant, or rhinocerus, gains considerable prestige amongst his fellows and, more important still, with the girls.

2. *Captains of the Warriors*

Every age-set in each district was under the control of a *nya-kangen* chosen for his prowess and powers of leadership, and although their selection was by popular acclaim, the chiefs generally took great pains to ensure the nomination of their own candidates, through whom their control was wielded. Nowadays the position is no longer filled, and chiefs frequently complained to me, when confronted with some unpopular task such as roadmaking or collecting tribute, that they could no longer control the warriors as their fathers had done, because there were now no captains to enforce discipline.

Theoretically the army consisted of four regiments (or drumships) organized on the kinship system, although they admit that, in fact, lads living in an area or district formed companies with their own elected officers, and the regiments were formed largely on a territorial basis. Usually only one drumship went to war at a time, and it was helped by volunteers from other drumships, eager for spoil. Thus the Kelenya are especially remembered for their wars with the Anuak, and the Ngarotti are said to have scored cheap victories over the Dinka, and avoided the stiff fighting engaged in by the other drumships. Whether this is truth or envy

I do not know, but today, of all the drumships, the Ngarotti have
the most cattle.

3. *The Order of Battle*

The order of battle was unvaried and everybody knew his station.
The Ngarotti and Ngenvac formed the right side when facing
their traditional enemies the Kum (the Tapotha, Karamojo, Jiye,
Turkana group of tribes), the Tangajon and Kelenya forming the
left side. The same relative positions were taken up if the enemy

BATTLE ARRAY

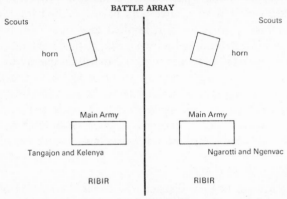

were the Jungkodh (Nuer and Dinka) to the north and west:
again the Tangajon and Kelenya formed the east side, with the
Ngarotti and Ngenvac on the west. These two sides, *ribir*, were
divided into the main army, *torobot*, and the horns, *oton*; the two
sets in the warriors' grade, strengthened by the set immediately
senior to them, formed the latter, while the three sets that were
still fairly active formed the *torobot* under the captain-in-chief,
nyakangen ci koodhu. Scouting or spying, *roten*, in which art they
were past masters, played an important preliminary part, and
provided young warriors with an opportunity to distinguish themselves by spying on the enemy, *arot modo*.

For some days before the warriors set out they formed into
parties and went begging, *marinet*, for food to strengthen them
for the tasks that lay ahead; and on full mobilization they repaired
to the drumchief for his blessing, as described in the previous
chapter.

There appears to be an interval of five or six years between the
different sets: after some ten years or so as a warrior, a man moves
up with his set to the next grade and a new set enters that of junior

warrior. The retiring warriors are then free to marry, settle down and raise families, drink beer, and use a stool, *lecar*. They still carry arms, and form the reserve of strength which may be called upon in an emergency: they are the village men until, with the lapse of time, they qualify for the elders' grade, *baicok*, who, instead of carrying arms, walk with a stick and use elaborate stools, *darkama*, which are usually three-legged. It is they, rather than the chiefs, who really rule the tribe according to customary law.

4. *Raids*

In addition to organized campaigns there were many raids by small parties of warriors, sometimes ten or twenty men, or even a pair of 'best friends'. These were known as *nyakwocom*, and stout-hearted warriors in the past captured many cattle by furtive attacks on Nuer and Dinka cattle camps, particularly the latter. Expert night-fighters, they undoubtedly captured considerable numbers of cattle from their Nilotic neighbours. The Kum[1] used similar methods and were therefore less profitable to raid.

Two of the greatest Murle experts at single-handed raiding were Ngaativoro and his 'best friend' Lokalio, both of the Kelenya drumship, who made innumerable attacks on the Anuak. Their amazing woodcraft enabled them to creep up to the Anuak villages at night, and overhear the arrangements for the following day. Stealthily and in darkness they slipped away to make their own plans. Lokalio, an old man with iron rings round his toes and ankles to commemorate the men he had killed, was still alive when I first arrived in the country; he was always given presents of fish and game, and the first fruits of the harvest, in acknowledgement of his former success. Ngaativoro died dramatically at the hands of the Anuak, throwing away his shield and spears and advancing fearlessly to his death unarmed, when all his party had been killed. Owing to a quarrel about the inadvisability of this raid Lokalio was not with him, and his sparring partner was too proud to return alone in defeat.

5. *Relations Between the Age-Sets*

A considerable bond exists between members of the same age-set, each set being expected to pay, and paying, great respect to senior ones. Each set has its own songs and adopts distinguishing

---

[1] Cf. p. 22.

badges and colours, *bayen ci bulu,* the animals or birds chosen as their mascots having the same colour conformation, and these introduce a lighter relief into their otherwise serious military purpose. The 'badges'—usually feathers worn on the head and bead patterns or other decorations on the body—all conform to the colour of a particular age-set, and with practise it is quite easy to distinguish one set from another. The colours of many sets are known, but it is only those of the junior sets which really count now, because they hold the dances. The Nyiridha, whose colour is, *budhen,* spotted, imitate leopards and guinea fowl, and also have a star dance.[1] Their badges are guinea-fowl feathers, worn on both sides of the head, white spots on their bodies, a leopard-skin belt, and blue and white beads arranged alternately. The Nyakademmo set, whose colour is white, *vor,* imitate the pelican and white cocks in their dances; their badges are a string of cowrie shells worn across their chests, *nyakalal,* white cocks' feathers on their heads, and white beads (with an odd red one to represent the red comb of the cock). The badges of the Tapaitho, who hold most of the dances, are black and white; they imitate the zebra, the golden-crested crane, and the colobus monkey in their dances; they wear the short black and white feathers of the *agmut*[2] bird on their foreheads, and a broad band of beads in black and white stripes across their chests; their dance shields—which are purely ornamental models, some 18 inches long—are generally made of black and white striped zebra skins. The Fartange, a very noted age-set in the past, used to wear giraffe-tail tassels above their left elbow, and the Kamuth a single nodding ostrich plume. The sense of unity between members of the same set—so strong that they may not marry each others' daughters—is reinforced by their songs and dances in imitation of their special animal or bird, in which members of other sets may not participate. The innumerable songs and stories of old battles and raids highlight the relationship between the existing age-sets, and although they refer to an age which is gone, they provide an essential part of the background of life as it is lived in their country today. Inevitably, relations with the sets immediately senior and junior are the closest, as at different times they share the grade of warriorhood, and in addition to the natural affinity resulting from shared tasks and pastimes, the sets are further linked by the institution of the 'best friend', *langdhet.*

---

[1] Cf. p. 49.   [2] *agmut* = golden-crested crane?

6. *The Institution of the 'Best Friend'*

Every man must have at least three *lango*, one in the set senior to his own, who is responsible for teaching him the arts of war; one in the junior set for whose military instruction he is responsible; and one in his own set, who 'shares his secrets'. The bonds between *lango* are very strong; they help each other in every possible way, frequently exchanging gifts of cattle. Special songs, *gutanin*, are sung in praise of the best friend, best friends hunt game together, and as far as possible share each other's lives. I was told that in the past *lango* could not be full brothers; and although it was permissible for half-brothers to be *lango*, or a man with the son of his maternal uncle, they were not usually related. 'If your best friend finds a lion you can fight it together, or a leopard or perhaps a buffalo, the pair of you can fight it: you fight the enemy together.' Once again the emphasis is on fighting, and the military basis of the institution is clear. If best friends belonged to different drumships, as was often the case, they would be separated in the order of battle, and if one was killed, the other frequently lost his own life in reprisal.

Driberg's account of the similar institution amongst the Didinga[1] shows that theirs corresponds closely with the Murle attitude:

Love of his best friend makes a warrior forget fear and forms a link between the different sets. If a man was found wanting in courage his best friend would be shamed and would reproach himself for not teaching him better. The importance of the instruction given by one set to that immediately its junior is always emphasized, and it was largely through the best friend that it was done. The relationship is stronger than that between full brothers or between a nephew and his maternal uncle and other kinship ties. Its great value in society as opposed to the personal aspect is the link which it affords between the different age-sets. The unity of each set is very marked and this link tends to counteract the exclusive classification by age which the age-set system otherwise makes.

7. *The Mowi Ceremony*

Another important rite of the age-sets that has persisted is the ceremonial killing of cattle, *mowi*. This is generally, but not invariably, held at the end of the rains in October, but it may be held several years in succession. Each drumship holds its own ceremony although, as a rule, only one set provides the oxen at a time. When

[1] J. H. Driberg, 'The "Best Friend" Amongst the Didinga', *Man*, 110 (July 1935).

I asked if all the warriors of the drumship were expected to fore-gather, they said 'Yes', but in the same breath qualified it by saying that if warriors were living in another district they could go to that ceremony if they wished. I gained the impression that, although, in theory, membership of a drumship depended on descent, every man being born into a clan and every clan belonging to one of the four drumships, in practice residence is the deciding factor. I have heard it said that it was to make the warriors strong before they left the villages for the grazing grounds, but as it is sometimes held in the early rains this is contradictory. Undoubtedly the killing of a warrior's name ox by his best friend, which should be done at the *mowi* ceremony of his age-set, is one of the reasons for the institution, but I suspect that the great importance attached to the ceremony today springs partly from the fact that it is the only occasion when the age-set system functions ceremonially in the present, except in so far as it controls dancing.

On initiation a young man's father gave him an ox, from which he took his bull name, and a cow with which to start his own herd: for all their mystical attachment to their cattle, the Murle are realists, and when an ox is fully grown there cannot be much delay before it is killed and eaten. During the period that a particular age-set occupies the position of senior warriors their celebrations are the main part of the ceremony: each set kills and eats its oxen separately, but the members of the senior warriors' set are expected to produce their special name oxen and to give their best friends the honour of killing them on the appointed day.

I found it very difficult to understand the *mowi* celebration: men were running in all directions, waving their spears, singing or shrieking wildly; from time to time one man would break off from the sham fighting and spear an ox, of which there were several running loose. The dead oxen were left lying where they fell until the late afternoon, when each set cooked and fed separately. Occasionally a set asked a man from a junior set 'to eat with [them] at *mowi*'—a great honour, almost equivalent to promotion (it is only done in the case of very important chiefs, or when a set has lost a very popular member through death, and asks his younger brother to take his place). In any case, it rarely happens before the sets concerned have attained the status of junior elder.

The significance of the ceremony appears to mark a transition from a period of comparative quiet, when the country was protected by the natural barriers of flood-water and swamp, to one requiring alertness for the defence of the country; and although this was never voiced, its close connection with the age-sets and drumships, and the particular emphasis on the institution of the 'best friend', seem to be logically implied. In any event, the practice affords revelry that appeals to such a cheerful people, it is anticipated with enthusiasm, and men spend hours preparing their hair beforehand—'Prick your heads' is the traditional formula sent round to warn people to prepare for *mowi*.

8. *Stick Fighting*

Age-sets still function through stick fights, *jore* or *ruon* (lit. 'quarrels'), which are stylized and highly conventional performances. The strength of the prohibition against the use of steel on another Murle, spears or wrist knives, *ngapel*, or knives, *kabath*, is very great, and such an attack rarely occurs, but of course, as in other societies, quarrels do happen. Amongst their Nilotic neighbours these lead to fights in which spears and rifles are used, but with the Murle such weapons are reserved for war, and are forbidden against fellow tribesmen: to fight with sticks, however, is a recognized and normal form of behaviour.

It is only witches and wizards who are considered to be so depraved and abnormal that they would disregard this prohibition concerning a fellow tribesman, and might use a spear if caught performing their nefarious practices; it is for this reason that they are so greatly feared.

There are two forms of stick fighting: between age-sets and between clans or other groups of kinsmen, but the technique is the same, and the same clothing is worn; they have a special cloak, *kabuli*, a tuft of lion's mane, *mah*, at the back of their necks, and wavy mud patterns drawn on their legs, often all over their bodies. Special leather greaves, *lotorkoc*, are worn on the arm and a small round shield or targe, *lotongkol*, is used to protect the hands. Frequently a chest-protector, *bokor*, made of a goatskin of the same colour combination as the owner's name ox, is also worn. Long, stout sticks, *dongka*, some five feet in length, or *nyideric*, which are shorter, are used, and men fight in pairs, standing at the ready with one foot advanced, their arms above their heads and the stick held vertically behind them. From this position they are exceedingly quick at parrying a blow from an opponent by a slight movement of their wrists, which serves to push their own stick forwards and to the left or right side, as the case may be. Downward blows are received on the targe or warded off with the stick; the great art is to be able to stop an adversary's blow and then slip in a quick jab before he has time to recover. Stick fighting between age-sets is often spoken of as *jore ci kumu*, *kumedhet*, or sometimes *myakiriam*; they are *ruon bulowa*, a 'fight of the sets'. They are generally provoked by some breach of etiquette on the part of a junior set. Fights between lineages may be caused by the cattle of one *korok* eating the standing grain of another, disputed ownership of fish, or the spearing of animals out hunting; these are known as *nyiila*.

Compensation is not paid for wounds given and received in stick fights, which serve a useful purpose in expending passion between angry groups. Serious wounds are seldom inflicted, because all taking part are very skilful in self-defence, and the underlying quarrel is usually settled afterwards at the club without any lasting ill feeling. At times quarrels lead to some *koroks* leaving the village for another, where they think they will find harmony with their neighbours: more often, however, the party adjudged in the wrong by the elders pays a beast of atonement, *mor ci dilento*, which is eaten by the latter, and the matter is closed.

9. *The Weapons of War*

War, *oron*, being the expression in action of the tension that persisted between the Murle, as a tribe, and the enemy, *modo*, was quite different. *Modo* includes all foreigners, and the capture of cattle or children from a neighbouring tribe was a highly laudable act of war; thus the distinction between *oron* and *ruon* is most marked in Murle thought. Their war weapons include the following:

Spears (general term)	*dila*
Broad-bladed spear	*nyatum*
Traditional Murle spear, used in most ceremonies, which is protected by a sheath	*giina*
Steel-hafted spear, said to have been introduced from the Kum	*nyaleero*
Short stabbing spear, particularly used at close quarters in night-fighting; also as a knife, if the latter is not carried	*nyatibut*
Broad wrist knife	*nyapel*
Spiked wristlet	*nyuany*

The *nyaleero*, *nyatum*, *nyatibut*, and *nyapel*, are always carried with narrow leather guards to protect their cutting edge. These are known as *nyakuraaro*, and the practice is also observed by the Taposa-speaking tribes, who also belong to the Nilo–Hamitic group. Murle shields, *kilip*, are small and oblong, with marked points at the corners; a black pompom of ostrich feathers, *nyakudhuri*, is generally worn at the bottom end of the wooden rib which runs down its length, providing the handgrip, *nyakoloket*, at the back. These are seldom more than three feet long, and frequently less, but the Murle, by half dropping (on one knee), were adept at taking cover behind them.

10. *Dances of the Drum*

In preparation for a dance the young men don their dance bells, *coren*, tie decorated belts, *nyakadengo*, round their buttocks, and put their feathers and beads on their heads; and in addition to their weapons some carry dance shields. When fully adorned they go to the dance floor, running in a long single line, *yitanin*, singing the songs of their age-set and practising various military manœuvres. This formation allows each set to display itself separately, and on the way to the dance floor the line visits each *korok* in the village, as an invitation to the girls and a signal for them to get ready. The leader, *et c'awo cowa*, or *et c'untane*, is a man practised in the movements, *aganek ludenet*, and the song leader, *et ci gitane* or *nawario*, is generally in the middle of the line.

The column members go round and round in ever-decreasing circles until they have all collected in the middle of the dance floor, still stamping round, and singing loudly, in a compact mass. After some minutes they break off, stick their spears in the ground near by, or lean them against a hut or tree, and then re-form round one edge of the floor in a long line facing the *nawario*. While awaiting the arrival of other parties from more distant villages, they sing and jump, *arogom*, keeping time by clapping their hands: gradually a long semicircle is formed round one side of the floor, with the junior set on the right and other sets in order of seniority to the left of them. Eventually the extremities meet, and as more people arrive the circle increases in size.

Meantime the girls prepare themselves. Their hair is dressed in butter-fat, *aluk oti*, sand, *kadhac*, and ashes from burnt grass, *tiring tiring*. They put on a broad band of beads across their foreheads.

nyaurit; a string of beads tied just above the eyes, *nyamaara*; and necklaces, *kalbe c'allemu*. They have long ropes of beads criss-crossed over their chests, *nyakilaalet*; armbands above the elbows, from which hang down thin strings of leather, having a knot at the bottom, *nyilaadet*, with which they flick the boys during the dance; above these, tied round their biceps, snippets from the tails of

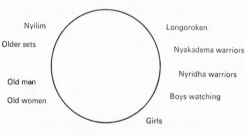

Diagram of Dance

Nyilim
Older sets

Old men

Old women

Longoroken

Nyakadema warriors

Nyridha warriors

Boys watching

Girls

Married women

lambs or small calves, *onyonu*; and a series of brass, copper, or white-metal bracelets, *nyagedhgedha*, on their wrists. Dance skins, *ngamedhac ci kurma-u*, are tied round their waists, which are embellished by leaving some of the hair in patterns; a small square apron is worn in front, *nyadhia*, decorated with cowrie shells and tassels (from the lower edge) strung with black beads; and, finally, they carry a broad band of beads, *kavale*, made into a belt: this is one of the most important pieces of the girls' attire, for it may be given to a special boy friend at the end of the dance as a mark of her favour and a memento. At the end of most dances two or three young men will be seen proudly wearing *kavale* round their necks. A warrior so adorned is thought to be inspired, and if he kills a dangerous animal, he will give the credit to the *kavale*, 'because it was not given to me for nothing'. Ear-rings too are very important. Women wear thick clusters of blue beads on wire rings, *nyagelwa*, but girls usually wear a single large white bead, *kalbe ci inu*. These beads, *kurdit*, are old, quite valuable, unobtainable in the shops, and are said to have been obtained long ago from the Galla (Ecumpa). If a girl gives one to her boy friend on a piece of giraffe-tail hair, he is high in her favour; and the effect of the *nyadhia* (apron) on the susceptible hearts of Murle warriors is said to be dynamic, making the girls far more attractive than in their normal scanty attire. When the girls are ready, they walk over to the dance floor in groups and take up their positions to the right of the married women.

A successful dance is not broken off until nightfall or, if started in the afternoon, may continue far into the night in the light of the moon. There are different phases of the dance; sometimes a set will sing and stamp in the middle of the floor, surrounded by girls who jump, *angoodh*, in a peculiar way that requires the help of two assistants. After a pause another set takes their place and acts a dance in imitation of one of the animals or birds of the age-set in question. Dances by the sets and individual performances by men or girls, popping in between the phases, are really only extras. The real dance, constantly repeated, is when the long line of men strikes up a song, marking time by clapping and stamping, and the girls sweep on to the floor and invite the man of their choice to dance with them by putting a foot on his *kolaan*. This is their great opportunity; the chosen partner leaves the line and starts jumping in front of the girl, who puts her hands lightly on his hips, and the pair jump all over the floor together. From time to time she flips him with the tassels hanging from her elbows, or ducks her head forward, hitting him on the chest with her hair. There is a good deal of jostling and bumping into each other, but the performers' faces are set and expressionless as they concentrate on the strenuous dance movements. After ten or fifteen minutes the singing stops and the performers return to their places. These dances, with their variations, are now being copied by the neighbouring Nuer and Anuak; many of the songs are sung in Tapotha, from whom much of the procedure is said to have been borrowed during the last few generations.

11. *Courtship*

Dances inevitably lead to flirting and courtship; if a girl wishes to know a young man better she will seek the assistance of her best friend; a boy will do the same, and a flirtation follows. This consists of the exchange of innumerable compliments and a great deal of caressing and pinching, and a special vocabulary is employed. There are no less than five recognized positions for sitting with a girl; *iren*, sitting side by side, with the boy's arm round the girl's shoulder; *abarcon*, lying or sitting side by side, facing in opposite directions, sometimes leaning back on each others' knees —this position is adopted particularly in the cattle camps, and the pair sometimes hug each other chest to chest; *nyaaginet*, the girl sitting on the boy's lap; *gula* lying down and reclining on one elbow facing each other, with one of the girl's legs over the boy's; *ong*, lying down facing, in the attitude of sleep, with arms around each other. This last position is used only after dark, and it is only if the girl has agreed to this intimate attitude that the boy will normally caress her vulva, *kabongkorot*. During flirtations both parties caress each other *um*, all over, and many boys and girls have patterns of raised scars, *longoditto*, on their shoulders, backs, chests, bellies, or thighs, to make this more intriguing. The patterns of scarification tend to vary between age-sets, according to current fashion. In addition to caressing and pinching, *wudiin*, there is kissing, *acoico*, which is the simple kiss, and the lover's kiss, *avoitet*, employing the tongue. By etiquette the boy is supposed to keep his private parts carefully tucked between his legs, and the girl is supposed to be annoyed if he has an erection, protesting: 'You want a woman, I am only a girl'; although, inevitably, intercourse occasionally takes place between a girl and her very special boy friend, the Murle maintain that it is rare, that some girls go to marriage as virgins, *ngan mot mot*, and that the favours of their girls are far harder to win than are those of Nuer and Anuak girls. To get an unmarried girl with child, *adule dole dhoc*—'to break a girl's leg' is the euphemism employed—is a very serious offence; the girl's kinsmen are entitled to come and beat the boy's kinsmen and his mother, the greatest indignity of all, and to kill his name ox, which should be preserved for sacrifice by his best friend at the *mowi* ceremony of his age-set. Although the child resulting from such a conception is known as a bastard, it will subsequently count as the legal heir of the girl's lawful husband. A girl who is anxious for her reputation will have only two or three boy friends at a time; a young warrior, on the other hand, is anxious to have as many girl friends as possible.

One of the most interesting features of Murle flirting is the words which are used only in love-making. These compliments, *redhonet* or *dithkak*, include the following:

Large-eyed	*lokonyen*
Thin flat-stomached	*neyeri*
Arch-backed	*gitun.*
Large-thighed	*lapandor*
Long-haired	*nettetim*

The hair at the back of a girl's head is dressed in a great number of tiny plaits, *kotir*, using only a few strands at a time; it is the length of these which is remarked on, because they swing when she is dancing.

Short-haired	*lomogor*
Slim-waisted	*lomeer*
Tall	*nagonga* (the everyday word is *wu-un*)
Short	*lawurien* (the everyday word is *kuttur*).
Slim	*dhaalac*
With pointed breasts	*tagoot*, or *keidhina tagoot* (lit. 'her breasts are giraffe-like')
Possessing spaced teeth	*longocel* (the normal word is *anyak alaato*)
Possessing an enlarged navel—regarded as a feature of great beauty	*logoto* (the normal word is *guldung*)
'Still, small, like an oribi's foot'—a great compliment, implying that the girl's vulva is still small	*ngan dhoc ci mageeru*
'Your tail is thornlike'—the corresponding compliment paid by a girl to a boy, referring to his thin penis with a long foreskin (whereas adult women prefer them large)	*en kul bilet*

The following refer to skin colours:

Copper-coloured	*likwang*
Red-tinged	*tebel*
Black and shiny	*koli wagirgir*

It will be noticed that the range of conventional compliments is sufficiently large to cover individual preferences, and that most people would qualify for several of them. The Murle sense of female beauty is much like other people's, they admire an erect slim-waisted girl with small pointed breasts, an arched back and straight legs; the real marks of beauty to them, however, are spaced teeth, an enlarged navel, and long hair: a girl with these is truly fortunate and will not lack for lovers. In addition to the conventional compliments an enthusiastic lover will devise special terms of endearment for his sweetheart, usually borrowed from those applied to animals.

VI

KINSHIP AND MORALS

1. *Kinship Categories*

As the homestead is the economic and social unit, so, in the sphere of kinship, is the family or household. It is referred to as the *ciedh*, the mother's hut, where she and her children live. It is felt that ideally a man should manage to marry four wives before he dies, and it is this polygamous family which provides the ideal pattern of life, with strict rules of seniority governing the status and behaviour of its members. There are four[1] categories of seniority (*abudhet*):

   i. for the wives of one man,
  ii. between full brothers (one mother),
 iii. between half-brothers (one father), and
 iv. [missing in author's manuscript. Logically this should be between sisters].[1]

The relationship between different members of the same category is seen to be unalterable. Specific designations within the various *abudhet* are: the first wife or brother is *abu*; the children of the first, second, intermediate, and younger wives are respectively *abunya*, *kanowaanya*, *korgenya*, and *toturnya*[2]; the sons of one mother stand to each other in exactly the same relationship; the eldest is the most important and is his father's heir; the youngest is the son of his mother's old age, and should be her prop and stay when she is too old to work, so that special emphasis is laid upon these two. The second brother acts for his elder brother should anything happen to him, so that this position is felt to be one of assistance or guardianship; the third or intermediate brothers are excluded from the duties falling to the first two and are, in some respects, the least important; they tend to be grouped with the youngest. Much the same duties and functions are felt to exist between the four households.

---

[1] Pp. 103, 106.
[2] Cf. p. 150.

Their definition of the polygamous family may be expressed by the following diagram, which is similar to that of the homestead.[1] The *abunya*, supported by the *kanowaanya*, are opposed to the *toturnya*, paired with the *korgenya*: this pattern of the whole organized in opposed pairs has, of course, been found in other facets of their organization; it is perfectly consistent with Murle thought.

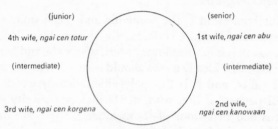

(junior) (senior)

4th wife, *ngai cen totur* 1st wife, *ngai cen abu*

(intermediate) (intermediate)

3rd wife, *ngai cen korgena* 2nd wife, *ngai cen kanowaan*

Although, as seen in Chapter II,[2] the polygamous family is the basis of the homestead, symbolizing, in its layout, the migrations of the tribe, each household has different connections through its mother, and is a separate entity in the sphere of kinship. A man's close cognatic kin comprise the following:

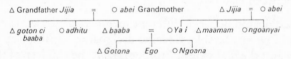

△ Grandfather *Jijia* = ○ *abei* Grandmother △ *Jijia* = ○ *abei*

△ *goton ci baaba* ○ *adhitu* △ *baaba* = ○ *Ya i* △ *maamam* ○ *ngoanyai*

△ *Gotona* Ego ○ *Ngoana*

It will be noted that the terms for an individual's uncles and aunts on the father's side of the family do not correspond with those on his mother's side: this becomes clearer in the next generation. On the father's side of the family the following terms are used:

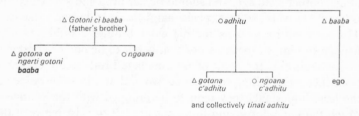

△ *Gotoni ci baaba* (father's brother) ○ *adhitu* △ *baaba*

△ *gotona* or *ngerti gotoni baaba* ○ *ngoana*

△ *gotona c'adhitu* ○ *ngoana c'adhitu* ego

and collectively *tinati aahitu*

The words father, *baaba*, mother, *yai*, grandfather, *jijia*, grandmother, *abei*, brother, *gotona*, and sister, *ngoana*, are all used in a classificatory manner: all paternal uncles are normally addressed as 'father' and great-uncles as 'grandfather'; cousins are usually referred to as brothers or sisters, although, if it is necessary to define the relationship more precisely, this is quite easily done by specifying whose children they are. In the same way half-brothers are spoken of as sons of one's father in distinction from the sons of one's mother:

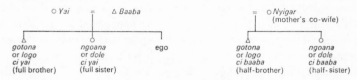

On the mother's side of the family the relationship terms are rather more complicated:

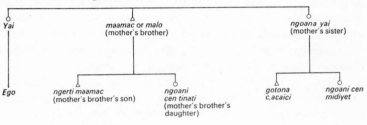

Thus it will be seen that all cross-cousins are included in the term *tinati*; the sons and daughters of one's father's sister and those of one's mother's brother. Cousins, children of one's father's brother, are regarded as classificatory brothers and sisters for whom there is no special term, although the children of one's mother's sister are *midiyet*, and one's mother's sister's son is a feud brother, *gotona c'acaici*, a relationship of especial significance.

The Murle consider the relationships existing between an individual and his cousins are *gotondhet*, or brotherhood, with the children of his father's brother; *adhitidhet* with those of his father's sister; *malotidhet* with those of his mother's brother, and finally, *ngoanidhet*, or sisterhood, with those of his mother's sisters. When allowance has been made for the generations, these are thought to be the fundamental relationships existing between all kinsfolk, and, once again, they are arranged in opposed pairs. Each relationship involves special reciprocal obligations, particularly in marriage and inheritance. In the predominantly patrilineal society the relationship of *gotondhet*, embracing the agnatic kin, is considered the most important, and it usually ranks before others within the family.

Relationship, *atendhet*, means that there are cattle, *ten*, between the people in question. When speaking of their agnatic kin the Murle say they are related like brothers, and that members of the same minimal lineage are *atenoc ci tinu*, referring to the cattle with which all members of the group are concerned when marriage is involved; members of the same lineage are *atenoc ci bordhetu*, and of the same clan *atenoc ci bangdhetu*. Thus there are three categories of agnatic kin: the minimal lineage, *tatok* (the word means the 'door of a hut', from which they believe all members of the group emerged), is the closest (*ciedh* is used symbolically for the family of the one woman who lives in the hut); *bor*, the lineage, is more distant, and the clan, *bang*, is the furthest removed. Every member of a clan is thought to be descended in the male line from a common ancestor, but the steps in descent have been forgotten. Fellow clansmen share in the use of inherited clan songs which are sung at marriages, but in little else, because they are now dispersed and without corporate existence. At the same time, it is said to be an advantage to belong to a large clan or numerous lineage, because clansmen tend to help each other and to exchange gifts in acknowledgement of the bond of kinship existing between them. For this reason a 'relationship of fish' is sometimes said to exist between clansmen, because they exchange presents of fish, whereas the relationship between members of the same lineage is closer and is marked by gifts of sheep, goats, or spears.

The interests of fellow members of a minimal lineage are more closely identified because they are all concerned in the cattle which are involved in marriages. Membership of the minimal lineage is normally counted from a man's great-great-grandfather: if the group is small, the relationship may be counted from a generation earlier, and if numerous, it may only be counted from the great grandfather, but this is a matter of convenience. That the agnatic principle is stressed is shown by the existence of these three gradations of relationship, because there are no equivalents for them in the other kinship categories used; within them an individual is said to be 'near' or 'far', much as, in our society, we speak of being closely or distantly related, but this is all. The emphasis on the agnatic kin therefore extends beyond the limit normally applied to the four categories of kinship.

The relationship of the agnates is particularly important in a family where the father has died or has no brothers. In this event, the father's sister has to ensure that the rights of his side of the family are not overlooked, in much the same way as the second brother is expected to act as assistant to his elder brother and guardian to his children if he dies. Her consent is always necessary to the marriage of one of her brother's sons or daughters. When cattle are to be shared, either after a marriage or by inheritance, she is particularly charged with the duty of preventing the mother from sacrificing the rights of her husband's family in favour of her own brothers; so there is always potential conflict between the *adhitidhet*[1] and the *malotidhet*. It is said that if a man died without heirs his mother's brother's people would come and take his cattle, but that if his father's sister were alive she would curse them, and they would be forced to return the cattle and admit their mistake: the Murle allege that this is because on marriage a girl's father's sister is entitled to a cow with a calf and an ox. Even great paternal aunts and their descendants are included in this relationship, and have a say in a man's or his sister's marriage; this is known as *adhituluren*, 'distant paternal auntship'. If, for example, a man is asked: 'Is she your own (or near) aunt, *adhitun wajon*?', he replies: 'No. She is not my real aunt, she is my kinship aunt, *adhitu cen lamurwac*, who was born with my ancestor. People have to pay cattle to the daughters of the daughters because they have eaten together for a long time. We respect her children who remain.' Such a man is trying to explain how many living people are included in the kinship category of the father's sister, although, strictly speaking, they are not true sisters of a man's father, but, by an extension of the classificatory system which is also applied to brothers, are held to come within its bounds.

It is the mother's brother, a correspondingly important relationship, who is expected to champion the rights of the mother's side of the family in any dispute with that of the father, and it is this function which sometimes leads to opposition with the group of the father's sister. He represents the agnatic principle in the

---

[1] *adhitu*, derived from *adhit* = 'hand' or 'arm'; *olc'adhitu* = 'the people of the hand', or 'the people of the father's sister', in Murle terminology; they assume, on his death, a jural role.

mother's family, as his name implies, *mai* or *mac* meaning 'male', and as appears in the word for the mother's brother, who is called *maamac* or *malo*. The sister's-son relationship, *ngirioanandhet*, is included in this category. The sister's son is expected to pay his mother's brother the greatest respect. He should spend a considerable part of his time in his mother's brother's homestead, and report to his mother when he returns on the welfare of her kinsmen. In this way the mother's side of the family shares in the education of her sons. Her brother is bound by tribal customs, which have the force of law, to help provide cattle when her son wishes to marry. Reciprocally, he is entitled to receive cattle when his sister's daughter marries. If he is rich, or has many daughters of his own, and provided there is harmony between the two families, and his sister's son has been dutiful towards him, he may contribute more than the minimum that he is legally obliged to provide. The generosity of a mother's brother to his sister's son is a theme often mentioned; it is felt to be obligatory, particularly if he used some of the cattle acquired by his sister's marriage for his own marriage.

Should a man's mother quarrel with her brother, it is a tragedy for her son, who is likely to forfeit his uncle's assistance, and may not even receive his rightful due; so it is a son's duty, and his own insurance, to foster good relations between his mother and her brother, and play his part in keeping the family together.

In the distribution of marriage cattle, and in inheritance, the category relationship of sisterhood[1] ranks as junior to the other three. In ordinary circumstances it is the least important, because society is normally patrilineal. The bond between cousins who have the 'sisterhood' relationship, however, is very important; it is said that 'they are like sisters because they are the sons of sisters'. They call each other *gotona c'acaici*, feud brother, which gives the clue to their relationship. 'A man cannot avenge his father', they say; 'his mother was bought with cattle, their blood is not the same, it is the feud kin, *ol ci caicinto*, who must avenge him, for their blood is the same.' Sometimes the term 'people of the womb', *ol ci momu*, is used instead, in which case the womb referred to is that of his mother's mother.[2] Kinsmen who are obliged to come to his assistance or avenge him are his kinsmen on the matrilineal line, led by his mother's brother.

---

[1] Cf. pp. 101, 103.   [2] Cf. p. 107.

2. The Institution of the Feud

The institution of the feud,[1] *caicinet*, is very interesting, because, in a tribe that is patrilineal in almost all other respects, it is organized on a matrilineal basis. A man's feud kin are those descended in the female line from his maternal grandmother. In Murle eyes they are all of the same blood, although not of the same lineage: they are, in fact, a blood-revenge group which has no corporate existence, unless and until some act occurs which brings them together into a state of feud with a similar group.

If a man is killed it is the duty of his feud kin to avenge him, either by killing the perpetrator himself, or a member of his feud kin, or by securing the payment of compensation. In the event of a man's killing another Murle, it is the duty of his feud kin to protect him from the attacks of the dead man's feud kin, to assist him in reaching sanctuary with the drumchief, and, finally, to assist him in obtaining the necessary compensation to be handed over to the dead man's kin by the chief. Once this is done the state of feud between the two groups is at an end.

Formerly compensation took the form of a child, either captured or bought from a neighbouring tribe. The Anuak were always prepared to sell a Masango child for ivory, and the Dinka frequently sold 'incest children' for cattle—these were children born of parents within the prohibited degrees of marriage, whose offspring, according to Dinka tribal law, should have been destroyed. The child, which should have been of the same sex as the deceased, took his place and name after being ceremonially handed over in compensation by the chief; this obtained even as regards inheritance and order of marriage in the family of the dead man. When this had been done, special ceremonies were held by the chief to end the state of feud between the two families, after which they could eat and drink together again in safety, without fear of death for the killer or one of his close relatives. For this reason, if a man was found dead in the bush and his kin suspected foul play, some of his bones were put into the nearest permanent water, in the hope that his killer or a close relative would drink of that water and die.

In 1943, when complaints were made about the Murle trade in Dinka 'incest children', the law of feud was altered, at a

[1] Cf. p. 78 et seq.

representative meeting of chiefs and elders over which I presided, by the substitution of the Nuer method of paying compensation in cattle. This system, which by providing cattle for the marriage of a wife to the ghost of the deceased, and so perpetuating his name, was accepted by the Murle at my suggestion, because the idea was not foreign to them: in a sense the principle of a life for a life was preserved.

The following diagram shows those kinsmen who, together, form an individual's blood-revenge group:

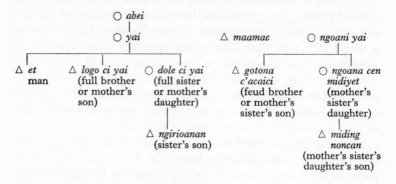

They are shown in three generations, corresponding with those normally alive together.

The institution of the blood-revenge group is thus consistent with the rest of Murle thought. It only comes into operation in exceptional circumstances: the normal, based on the patrilineal structure of society and, in particular, on the agnatic category of kinship who share the relationship of brotherhood, is contrasted with the abnormal, which invokes the matrilineal principle of the blood-revenge group and, in particular, those kinsmen who had the relationship of sisterhood. The analogy with the pattern of relationships between wives is completed by the opposition shown to exist between the kinship categories of brotherhood and sisterhood. Diagramatically it may be expressed by arranging the four recognized categories of kinship as follows:

Mother's side of the family	*Father's side of the family*
Mother's brother's group	Father's brother's group
Mother's sister's group	Father's sister's group

Mother's brother's group ⟩ ⟷ ⟨ Father's brother's group
Mother's sister's group ⟩ ⟷ ⟨ Father's sister's group

3. *Inheritance and Property*

An adult normally calls any child related to him 'my boy', *logocan*, or 'my girl', *dolecan*, in conformity with the usual practice of addressing a kinsman by using a closer term than that to which he is strictly entitled. This is a form of politeness, for it is correct behaviour or good manners to show respect to one's kinsfolk, and at the same time to emphasize the unity of the family. If, in conversation, parents wish to stress the fact that it is their own child they are speaking of, the father uses the word *ngeran*, which has the connotation of 'son and heir': derived from the verb to 'divide', it signifies the eldest son, who will ceremonially divide the cattle between his father's heirs on his death. All children share in their father's inheritance, but it is the first-born, the eldest son of the senior wife,[1] who inherits the headship of the family and is a man's real son and heir, *ngeran c'ateyana*, 'my divider of my cattle'. A mother speaks of her daughter as 'my blood', *benyan*, thus implying that her daughter has inherited her mother's blood, which she will transmit. The following table shows the terms used:

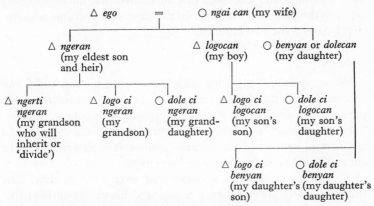

Grandchildren are spoken of collectively as *dole-ci-dolecu*, literally the 'children of the daughters', and sometimes *dol-u-dol-ugan*, the 'seed of our seed'. Other derivations of these basic terms are used to express precise relationships of various children, classificatory children, or grandchildren, although 'my boy's boy' or 'my girl's girl' are considered adequate for ordinary purposes.

Another term, *beniet*, expresses the relationship existing between

---

[1] Cf. p. 101.

the various daughters of the family; it exists between a man's own daughters, his sister's daughters, and even between the daughters of his half-sisters, children of his co-wife, but I was never able to discover its functional significance, except as an extension to classificatory daughters.[1]

Murle society is exogamous, and in principle sexual intercourse with any 'daughters of the clan' is forbidden. In practice, although the rules of exogamy are more strictly observed in the chiefly families than by commoner-clans, the prohibition does not extend beyond the patrilineal lineage, and, as a rule, it is not regarded as serious beyond six generations of ascent. In the other lines of ascent—a man's mother's clan, his two grandmothers' clans, and those of his four great-grandmothers—the prohibition is less important still, and ends after four generations, which is as far as Murle can remember. This attitude toward exogamy is consistent with the special stress laid on the agnatic kin in other respects, but before any marriage can take place the elders and old women of the two families concerned have to take precautions by recounting their ancestors and marriage ties, to ensure that no impediment exists to the proposed marriage on the score of a previous relationship between the two families.

4. *Incest*

Incest, *ngilidh*, is regarded with the greatest horror, and I was repeatedly told that in the past the offence was almost invariably punished by death. This extreme repugnancy, of course, refers to 'incest with a sister', which is the worst form of the offence, and includes all manner of classificatory sisters. It is also relative—the closer the relationship the more heinous the crime—but, in spite of the horror it inspires, it does occur from time to time. The trouble usually arises between a man and his sisters-in-law; that is to say, women with whom there is no bar on account of their descent, but only because they have married some elder kinsman of the man's, which brings them to live in his homestead, or one which he visits frequently. This is recognized as less serious than incest with a blood relative, because if the kinsman in question died, the offender might be chosen to raise up seed by the woman in question to his kinsman's name. Nevertheless, even this milder

[1] Cf. p. 105.

Incest

form would probably be punished, if detected, by disinheritance and expulsion from the family, and if repeated after atonement had been made, would be regarded in the most serious light. The taunt of *ngilidhoc*, the adjective applied to one who has committed incest, is a dangerous one, and one of the worst insults that can be uttered, for, if proved, the charge implies the death penalty, and the scorn has been known to lead to suicide: hanging appears to have been the method of execution used in both cases.

5. Marriage

Relationship by marriage, *kaavdhet*, is considered most important, and the respect paid to parents-in-law is very marked: men are always addressed as 'father', whatever their age, thus being accorded the respected status of a senior generation, and women as 'mother'. There is a special word for mother-in-law, *inyik*, but other relationships are expressed by using the ordinary kinship terms with the addition of *cen kaav*, 'in-law'. A man uses the following terms:

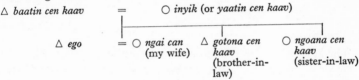

Special terms for her new relatives are employed by the wife, who usually goes to live in her husband's homestead, where she is spoken of as 'daughter-in-law', *alowan*:

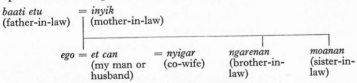

A son-in-law should respect his mother-in-law in order to earn her good opinion. If he sees her coming he should sit down and tuck his private parts between his legs. If she comes to his homestead he should put a skin over his shoulders, sometimes with a belt tied round it, to cover his nakedness. He should talk as little as possible in her presence, conduct her to the place of honour in the coolest part of the hut, and see that she is provided with everything she needs. In this way he hopes to secure her support with his wife, for it is believed that 'sons follow their fathers, daughters their mothers', and if a son-in-law succeeds in winning his mother-in-law's esteem, she will tell her daughter to look after him well, and discourage her from seeking divorce. Conversely the mother-in-law is expected to show respect for her son-in-law by avoiding him; if she sees him first, she should sit down. The son-in-law is not allowed to eat food that she has cooked, although frequently she sends her daughter flour that she has ground, or fat, telling her that she must feed her husband well.

Any suggestion of sexual intercourse between son-in-law and mother-in-law is regarded as particularly shameful: it is thought that the act would have dangerous consequences for those closely related to them, and certainly cause the young man's wife to become barren. The only case I heard of caused an outrageous scandal, for the mother-in-law was popularly regarded as being the chief culprit. Her enraged daughter, who caught them, divorced her husband, who was so laughed to scorn by his neighbours that he left his village and went to live far away in the extreme western corner of Murleland.

6. *Bridewealth*

The kinship system functions most clearly in marriage when the reciprocal obligations find expression in the transference of cattle and other gifts. Besides being a union between man and woman, marriage is also an alliance between the families of the bride and bridegroom, between whom it creates a new series of kinship ties. The girl's family loses a member, and the balance between the two families is restored by the cattle which leave the homestead of the bridegroom's father and join that of the bride's father.

Enthralling hours are spent discussing the collection and division of the cattle involved, for although the process is governed by custom there are individual differences to be taken into account in every marriage before the whole transaction is complete.

The underlying principle is that four categories of kin each contribute on the husband's side, and receive on that of the bride, as shown below:

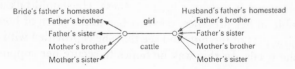

Bride's father's homestead		Husband's father's homestead
Father's brother	girl	Father's brother
Father's sister		Father's sister
Mother's brother	cattle	Mother's brother
Mother's sister		Mother's sister

Inevitably the individuals comprising the father's brother's group of kin vary in every family, and it is the same with each of these kinship groups. In addition to this complication, every marriage is one of a series and cannot be understood in isolation. The seniority of four brothers of the same mother is simple, and they are married in the order of their birth, but the seniority between half-brothers, *abudhet ci baatidhet*, the 'seniority of paternity', is more intricate, because in practice the order of birth does not correspond with the theoretical order of seniority. The principle is important, however, in the case of the eldest son of the senior wife, the heir to the headship of the family, and between half-brothers who are age-mates and therefore hope to get married at much the same time. In this event the available cattle on the father's side of the family—for the members have different mothers—have to be devoted to the marriage of the brother who ranks senior, according to this rule, in the whole polygamous family.

The same principle, in reverse, is seen in the case of three sisters of the same mother: when the first is married it is said that her father will have to distribute practically all the cattle which fall to the share of the agnatic kin to members of his minimal lineage. On the marriage of his second daughter he will probably still have to hand over the majority of the cattle; by the time his third daughter is married, however, he should have succeeded in meeting his obligations to all kinsmen in this category, and so be able to keep most of them for himself, merely meeting a few outstanding claims from junior members of his lineage who failed to get their share of the two previous divisions. The father always tries to give cattle to as many fellow members of his lineage as possible, because they are then bound to help in providing cattle when his sons come to be married. So the obligations of kinship are determined in any particular marriage by promises given at previous marriages with which the group was concerned, or by promises given at the time of the marriage under discussion, to meet outstanding obligations at some future marriage of one of the group. If, for example, the bride's father has several sisters, they cannot all expect to receive their due from one marriage: the senior sister of the bride's father has the first claim, her younger sisters having to wait until one of the bride's younger sisters is married. So it is with the other kinship groups: the rules of family seniority always come into play; some claims are met at the time, others postponed for later settlement, although promises are made, and invariably the senior members of any group are the first to be paid.

Certain claims are now more or less standardized, although they cannot always have been so, because the number of cattle transferred has varied considerably over the past sixty years. The senior man of the bride's extended family of minimal lineage, *abu ci boru*, always receives a cow because he is responsible for the division of the cattle. The bride's mother is given a cow with its calf and a large ox, both the bride's grandmothers receive an ox and a large ram, and the paternal grandmother may receive a cow and a calf as well. The bride's father's sister is entitled to at least a large ox, and expects a cow with its calf, if not more. The bride's mother's brother will claim the same, but will in fact receive less. When these demands have been met, the remaining cattle go to meet the claims of the agnatic kin, and any left over after this are disposed of by the father of the bride. The method of settling these claims is illustrated by the following examples:

Cangkac married his first wife in 1904 for sheep and goats; he later married Kotobot, his second wife, for sheep and goats; she bore him two daughters who were eventually married for seven and eighteen cattle respectively. Later ten cattle were paid to Kotobot's parents to complete her bridewealth. His third wife, Alaten, was exchanged for ten sheep and goats and some grain; after the birth of her second son ten head of cattle were paid to her parents to complete the transaction. His fourth wife was married for sixteen cattle, and her son married a girl for twenty-four cattle in 1946. Cangkac's sixth wife was married for five cattle, and on her daughter's marriage cattle will have to be paid to her parents. His seventh wife was married for eighteen cattle, and his eighth for fifteen.

Another example showing the gradual increase in the number of the bridewealth cattle is provided by Kengen Baatalan's five marriages, which involved five cattle in 1904, ten in 1910, twelve in 1924, fifteen in 1931, and fifteen in 1943.

In recent years pretty girls of good family have been married for thirty cattle or more, depending on the individual circumstances of the bride and bridegroom and their families. The bride's parents are always at pains to point out, during the negotiations, that they have numerous kinsfolk whose claims will have to be met, although it is fully realized that, if their demands are too exorbitant, discussions will flounder, and as kinship obligations are reciprocal they do not normally wish this to happen. Their own family and lineage have sons who will want to marry and beget children to carry on the line, and all who look to receive cattle on the marriage of a daughter of the group will have to contribute towards the marriage of sons; so that, although there is great scope for haggling, it is balanced by a measure of group responsibility, and a common aim on both sides, which usually ensure successful negotiations.

It is recognized that marriage for bridewealth in the form of cattle would not work if it were restricted to a single household, because in that case a son could marry only with the cattle provided by his sister's marriage, and a boy with several sisters would be considered fortunate. The system of bridewealth undoubtedly provides a valuable element of stability for the marriage, for the woman's kin will have to hand back any cattle they received, with their progeny, if the marriage is subsequently dissolved, and it is, therefore, in their own interests to do all they can to make the marriage a success and dissuade the bride from neglecting her wifely duties.

7. *Negotiations for Normal Marriage*

When a young man's age-set has completed its time in the warriors' grade, his thoughts normally turn towards marriage, and as the position of the senior wife is so much more important than that of her juniors, the choice of his first bride concerns his family greatly, and his mother is almost certain to have strong views on the subject. She is mainly interested in the girl's character and capabilities: whether she is a good cook and worker in the fields, whether she comes of a good family and has a reputation for being respectful to her seniors, and whether the women of her family are fruitful. The young man is inevitably far more interested in her personal charms and attainments in dancing, and often has to seek the assistance of his maternal uncle in persuading his mother to accept the girl of his choice.

From proposal to consummation the process of marriage is a lengthy affair, and although I have looked into a hut where marriage talks were taking place, I could see little more than an over-filled hut, crammed with humanity, and can make no claim to have seen the full marriage ceremony. The following is an almost literal translation of an account of one recorded for me by one of my

Murle assistants. It is given here because it expresses in their
own way the important phases of the prolonged negotiations involved:

'I want to get married, I will go and ask the girl.'

The people say: 'She is related and is going to marry somebody else;
you can go and find another girl.'

'I will go and find this out; I will ask the girl.'

The people say: ' "So-and-so" is still white (unmarried), the daughter
of "So-and-so", good people who are not related to us.'

'I agree, I will marry this girl; let us start.'

The people say: 'Go with your "best friend" and talk to the girl.'

The girl asks: 'Is this marriage talk?'

The boy replies: 'Yes, flirting itself, with beads.'

The girl says: 'I am betrothed, the man of my choice is not you,
I don't want you.'

The boy goes on talking to the girl for many moons, and then she
says: 'Yes. I want you yourself. I myself have agreed on you.'

The boy says: 'We have both agreed; let us run away together.'

The girl refuses. 'No we will not elope; go to my father and my
mother; all my mother's cattle have not yet been paid.'

'Good', replies the boy. 'This is good talk, but you are not deceiving
me? If I go to your mother tomorrow you will not refuse to come?'

The boy goes to the girl's mother and says: 'You bore me (a very
polite way of greeting her). I want your daughter.'

She replies: 'I have no daughter.'

The boy says: 'But you have a daughter, mother. I have seen her,
a girl called "So-and-so".'

'Indeed', replies the woman. 'Then we will discuss the matter at
length. Good. You are always troubling me about my daughter, I have
heard you: come and talk it over. I have agreed. Go to your father, tell
him I sent you; let him come and see me. What do you say? There
(indicating her relatives) are my mothers' (a polite way of referring to
them).

'I have heard', says the boy, who returns home and tells his father.

Then the people go to the marriage talks. The man tells his wife to
put fat on the boy's head and their own; the people prepare their hair
with pins, so that it sticks out, and go to the talks. The boy ties on his
beads. The man comes, and goes to the talks with the men of his
lineage. When they go they sing praises and the women trill. The girl's
kinsmen take all the skins, they take them to the hut of the man who is
senior to them all. They all go and enter the house of the senior man.
The man who came wanting a girl is singing praises in the homestead;
he comes and enters the house, and tells the senior man the colours of

the cattle, both milch cows and oxen. The senior man is pleased; he lies down on the ground and tells his kinsmen to talk with the man. The head of the second household in the girls' homestead numbers the cattle, perhaps twenty or so.

'Now,' he says, 'it is good; go back home, let us think it over; tomorrow we will come and number the cattle mentioned yesterday.'

They agree. After many visits they agree, and the people say to the senior man 'This is what we say.'

He beats the skins on which he is sitting with his hand; the people hide the armpit cowbell at first, then they give it to the senior man; he puts it on, rings it, sings praises, and when he stops he beats the skin again. The people who want the girl say 'What do you say?'

The girl's people reply: 'What do you want?'

The boy's people say: 'We want a wife.'

The girl's people reply: 'Sit down here.'

They then beat the skins again and start singing their songs. They sing for a long time; they sing all round the homestead until they come back to the house. Then all the people talk together for a long time about things of long ago. In the late afternoon the boy's people say: 'Father, we will go home now.'

They sing the clan songs again, then they go straight home. On the way they keep silent, but when they reach their own homestead they sing their clan songs again. They go to the senior man's hut; he takes a ram, they kill it with a stick; he tells them: 'I am tying the girl with this sacrifice', and he puts some of the fat round her neck. She stays four or five days. Then the senior man of the boy's family sends her home. 'Go and tell your father I will come tomorrow morning early. I will "beat" the cattle all together.'

Then the people sing the clan songs; they are sitting in the senior man's hut; they come out, the senior man goes in front and the people stay with the cattle between them. They send for the elders, who ask the people who have brought the cattle: 'How many cattle have you brought?' (lit. 'The ox you have brought has now many fingers?')

The boy's people reply: 'We have brought the marriage cattle, twenty-three of them.'

The girl's people say they are disappointed, and ask for others.

The boy's people tell the colours of two more, and the people say: 'Good.'

They go into the house and start singing the clan songs. The girl's people take some coffee, *meo*, and the people drink it. The boy's people give another sheep to the senior wife; they say: 'We have covered the coffee pot's mouth.'

They bless the girl and put the firesticks on her knees. They give

her half a gourd and an axe, so that she can build her man a house.
Then the people take the girl home; they say: 'Father, may we go and
look after our own affairs?'

They sing the clan songs once more: the people take their wife home.

This account is slightly foreshortened, because there is, of
course, a good deal of variation between marriages, but in discussion with them it is clear that the Murle distinguish the following stages. First, the proposal, *ronginet* (and the difficulties which
may occur are indicated in the account above); second, the negotiations, *tinkawin*, which may take many days spread over several
months; third, the betrothal, signified by the *abu* of the girl's
family swearing on the cow hide on which he sits, and ringing the
hereditary armpit cowbell. This vow is completed by the girl's
paying a short visit with her 'best friend' to the boy's homestead,
where a sacrifice is made, and she is 'tied', *acap*, with some of the
fat from this offering. The promise is normally ratified a few days
later by the transfer of the first cattle: there is often a pause then,
before the final ceremony. This consists of three distinct parts:
ceremonial coffee-drinking, *awut meo*; blessing the bride, *mayuwanet*; taking her home, *vecinet*. Ritual coffee-drinking is an essential part of the ceremony,[1] and as there is no coffee in Murleland
it has to be imported from Boma or Ethiopia; great stress is laid
on the antiquity of the custom. It is the privilege of the senior
woman of the girl's family to brew the coffee, for which she
receives a sheep, and the resulting concoction is often so bitter
that it makes everyone sick: this is taken as a good omen. Blessing
the bride is also important. She sits down on the ground with her
legs straight out in front of her; the bridegroom sits immediately
behind her with his legs on each side of her: the sacred firesticks
are put on her lap, and the pair are then blessed through the sprinkling of water from the special gourd by the senior man of her
family, who counsels her to bear many children, to cultivate
assiduously, and to feed her husband well. A piece of wood is cut
off the sacred firesticks and given to her, which she afterwards
wears on a string around her neck. She is then given an axe, a
gourd, a sleeping hide, some mussel shell spoons, and possibly
other household utensils.

Vecinet is carefully timed so that the party will reach the

[1] Cf. p. 151.

bridegroom's homestead just before dark. The girl, accompanied by her 'best friend' and other female relatives, carries her husband's spear on her head, and great pains are taken to ensure that the party meets nothing ill omened on the way. That night the bride and bridegroom and both 'best friends' sleep in a hut which has been specially prepared. It is not until at least the second night that the newly wedded pair are left alone to sleep together. Some three or four months after her arrival the wife is given new skins by her husband's family, and dressed as a married woman; even then she has to wait for a year or two before being given the characteristic white belt, *voco*, of a married woman. This happens when, at the next early rains, she and her husband have built themselves a new hut—the main part of this work is hers—and cleared their own patch in the millet plot of the homestead. Until her hut is built the bride generally lives in that of her mother-in-law or the senior woman of the homestead, so that she may be properly instructed in the duties of a wife.

8. *Division of Marriage Cattle*

The scale of entertainment provided for the visiting kinsmen varies a good deal, according to the wealth of the families concerned, but is always considerable when the first cattle, ratifying the betrothal, are paid, and when the bride is taken home.

Once the bride has left with her new husband's people, the marriage ceremony is concluded for her own family by the division of the cattle, *kulin*. This is another lengthy affair, performed by the head of her lineage in the father's homestead. Here again details vary, as clans do not all have the same custom in this respect, but the essential features do not alter.

The main conference is held in one of the huts of the homestead, everybody sitting on the mud floor, except the head of the lineage, who sits on a skin. Everyone present presses his own claims, and from time to time the head of the lineage has to exert his authority. In fact, it is the head of the lineage and the *et ci kanowaan*, the senior representative of the descendants of the second household in the lineage group, who, with the bride's father, decide on the disposition of the cattle. In the event of dissension the head of the lineage threatens that he will refuse to bless the cattle, and that the ancestral spirits will therefore be displeased. Eventually, after much discussion, he calls for some special grass and the sacred firesticks: the grass is lit and charred to ashes, and he calls for some fat and milk from the cattle concerned. This is put into the sacred gourd with which the bride's father, or the head of the homestead if he was living in that of another man, blessed the cattle on their arrival. He spits on them, anoints himself in the customary manner, and then passes the fat, milk, and ashes to the *et ci kanowaan*, who must be sitting on his left. The latter anoints himself, blackening his face with the ashes, and exhorting the ancestral spirits of the lineage to bless the division. As the day draws on the head of the lineage blesses the bride's mother. He calls for a skin and puts it on her, rings the sacred armpit cowbell, hangs it round her neck, and the group then sing the family songs. This may continue for an hour or so, but at length the head of the lineage gets to his feet, followed by everyone else. He makes as if to go out of the door, but at the last moment steps back, causing everyone behind him to jump backwards to get out of his way; this is repeated several times before he finally leaves the hut. He then calls for a bunch of *nyalli* grass and an ox, a cow, and a calf from the bridewealth. He strikes each of these beasts twice with the grass, calling on many of those present and telling them to go away. Eventually, late in the afternoon, he takes the inherited spear of the family, and dons his black-and-white colobus-skin armlet, *dore ci karamu* (both of which are carefully preserved in the homestead for special occasions); the wearing of these is said to be a very old custom. As there are now no colobus monkeys in their country, they are obtained from Boma.

Ultimately the head of the lineage taps a beast with the spear, shouting: 'So-and-so, that's yours', and quickly moves on to the next, until the whole herd is disposed of. It is a typical Murle ceremony, at which the ancestral spirits are invoked, the rules of family seniority come into play, and the bonds of kinship are expressed in the transfer of cattle, after the customary mystical precautions against evil have been taken.

Nowadays, when the formal division of the cattle has been completed, the boy's parents almost invariably hand over two 'secret' cattle to those of the girl as a final pledge between them. This is not part of customary law, and so is not mentioned during the division of the cattle, although everyone present knows that it will take place.

9. *Other Forms of Marriage*

There are three other modes of marriage. The first, *tiken*, is appropriate where the young couple elope. When this is discovered, the girl's family summon their kinsmen, who dress up for stick fighting, and repair to the boy's homestead, where they angrily demand the return of their daughter and threaten to seize all the cattle in the homestead if she is not produced immediately. The boy's family hastily send for reinforcements from their kinsmen, and to neighbouring elders to come and mediate.

A fight may ensue, or, if the boy's family is rich in cattle and recognized as worth marrying into, the elders may find a basis of agreement. In the latter case, the clan songs will be sung, and the girl's family will drive off the cattle and tell the boy to bring the girl back to her father's homestead for her traditional blessing, in a few days' time. When he does so, the marriage is completed with the ceremonial drinking of coffee together by the two families, after which the bride is conducted to her husband's homestead in the appropriate manner.

Yowanet, when the girl takes the 'bit between her teeth' and runs off to the homestead of her young man, occurs comparatively rarely. It usually leads to a fight or a serious quarrel between the two families, because one of them is almost always strongly opposed to the marriage. Sometimes a girl's parents have tried to arrange a marriage for her to a man she does not wish to marry: he may be old and rich, or belong to a particularly desirable family with which they wish to be connected. This mode of marriage, for it is recognized as such, gives her the chance to marry the man she loves. Sometimes, it is said, girls prefer to commit suicide when their families are very importunate, rather than marry against their will. Genuine 'elopement by the girl' is rare, although young men who are unwilling to face their families' anger in normal elopement may try to persuade the girl to elope as a means of overcoming the delays and difficulties involved in normal marriage.

The third mode, *dongin*, from the verb 'to carry', sometimes occurs when a girl child has been pledged as a future wife by her family, in return for a first payment at the time of her betrothal, to tide the family over some difficulty. In such cases the girl is ritually carried to her future husband's homestead at the time, but may well object when she grows up, and elope to secure the man of her own choice.

In addition to these recognized forms there also occur levirate marriage, and two forms of ghost marriage. If a man dies young leaving a widow, she should go on living in her dead husband's homestead and raise children to his name. Ideally she should cohabit with her late husband's half-brother, or any reasonably close kinsman of the same lineage. Provided that she lives in their homestead, her husband's family are not likely to grumble seriously if she takes a lover outside his agnatic kinship group, because legally the children will be the 'children of the cattle', since the widow still has 'cattle on her back', and these will count as her late husband's children.

If a man or boy dies before he has married, his next full brother in order of seniority should marry a wife to his brother's name, before marrying a wife for himself, and the children begotten by this wife will count as the heirs of his dead brother; only when he has married his own wife can he beget children in his own name. If there is no younger brother, the dead boy's family should find some other kinsman to undertake the duty for their dead son: this is known as the 'dead boy's marriage', *rocen logo c'adai*.

From this it will be seen that more importance is attached to the legal paternity of a child than to the physical fatherhood. This concept is further exemplified in the institution known as daughter-in-law marriage, *alowan ci nga-u* (lit. the 'wife's daughter-in-law'), for the Murle contend that if a wife has failed to bear a male child the line cannot be allowed to die out, and a wife must be married to the child she failed to bear. It is not regarded as the marriage of woman to woman, but as that of a woman to the imaginary son she would have borne, but for the intervention of some evil. Diagramatically this could be expressed as follows:

If a man A marries a wife B, her imaginary male child X should grow up and marry Y who would then become the daughter-in-law of A and B. Y's children by X should become the heirs of A in the second generation, and particularly so if B was his senior wife. If A has a son D by his second wife C, he should act for his non-existent half-brother X and beget a boy Z by X's wife to Y's name, who will inherit the headship of A's family.

$$B \quad = \quad A \quad = \quad C$$
$$X = Y \qquad D$$
$$Z$$

This form of marriage is not as rare as might be expected, and when speaking of a daughter-in-law of this kind the Murle say: 'She can speak loudly to the men and tell them what to do', because her theoretical husband (unborn) is the senior son and her first born, who will one day become head of the family.

10. *Adultery and Unlegalized Unions*

There are, in addition, a certain number of men and women living together in unlegalized unions. If a widow, *ngai ci boi*, fails to beget a child after living for a time with her late husband's brother, or other nominated kinsman, she will probably form an attachment with another man. In a polygamous society there are plenty of widows of rich men who are still comparatively young when their husbands die; other women have deserted their husbands but not yet been divorced, and if they 'join up' with another man they are referred to by the second man's relatives as 'another man's wife', *ngai c'ulu*, or a 'woman who is sitting', *nga c'avtidh*, meaning that she is living in the homestead in an unlegalized union. There are, too, always a few divorced women who have not yet remarried, in which cases the woman will probably marry the man with whom she lives in temporary union, particularly if he begets a child by her and has sufficient cattle for her bridewealth. It is with these unattached women, widows, divorcees, and deserters, that the warriors and young unmarried men, *moldong*, enjoy their sex life. Their attentions are by no means confined to these unattached women; all of them have affairs with the young married women as well. I was told that more than half the young married women are unfaithful to their husbands, and that no man with more than two wives could expect them to remain faithful. A number of factors together produce this state of affairs. The comparatively late age at which the men marry is one; few of them do so before they are twenty-eight or thirty, and during the ten years or so while they are warriors they have numerous flirtations. A girl who has refused their advances before she is married, for fear of conception, is afterwards often only too anxious to accept them. If her husband is old or absent, or sleeping with another wife, 'what more natural', they say, than that she should seek solace in the arms of one of her former friends, particularly as the penalties for adultery are not usually serious. Admittedly, if a young woman acquires the reputation of promiscuity, *wangnyai*, she may be divorced, but provided she can bear a child she need not fear lack of a husband.

The great variation in wealth between families means that a significant number of men never succeed in making a legal marriage: they are known as *barin*—a term of considerable opprobrium —and the greatest tragedy that can befall a Murle is to have no kin to perform for him the last rites on his death. *Barinya* (pl.) are dragged out into the bush by their heels when dead, and the fear of this indignity causes a lad with few relatives to lament bitterly that he is an orphan, *boyoi*. Conversely rich men have more wives than they can satisfy sexually, and the younger of these encourage 'bachelors of the night', *barinya ci balinu*. The old men complain bitterly that in their young days they were so busy serving as warriors in the protection of their country that they had little time for affairs of this nature.

A husband who is impotent, *ilelli* or *tarlen*, or sterile, *nyakaluk*, will tell his wife to take a lover in order to 'find a child in the bush'. There is a distinction between this illegitimate child and a bastard, *bidhir*: a child born to an unmarried girl is a *bidhir*, although when she marries it will be legitimized and become her husband's legal progeny; however, in a quarrel in later life the fact might react on the child. Children born in legitimate wedlock, and the physical children of their legal father, are also referred to as bastards if their mother is divorced and subsequently remarried, although they will count as the legal children of their mother's second husband. Children born to a man's wife as the result of an illicit affair with another man, or 'found in the bush' after his own death, are nevertheless his legal children, and the term *bidhirnya* cannot be applied to them.

The following figures should be treated with some reserve, as they were collected in March 1949. They concern the state of affairs that obtained during the 1948 rains, during the time of year when village life may be regarded as most normal; at least they give some idea of the relative frequency with which the various forms of marriage or unlegalized unions occur.

Amongst the 81 women living in Kavacoc village I heard of 17 who were married by elopement and 5 by child marriage—the remaining 59 presumably being married by normal procedure. Of these 81 women, 11 were living as widows in their late husbands' homesteads; 2 were the daughters-in-law of barren wives, and

4 were divorced and living in unlegalized unions. Among the 151 women living in the three Veveno villages I was told of 6 marriages by elopement, 8 daughter-in-law marriages, 2 girls' runaway marriages, 2 child marriages, 3 levirate marriages, and 1 ghost marriage. Of these women 17 were living as widows in their late husbands' homesteads and 2 in unlegalized unions. Of all marriages in Murleland, I think an estimate of 10 per cent by elopement and 7 per cent by child marriage would be near the truth. *Yowanet* would probably prove to be less than the 1 per cent of the example; daughter-in-law marriage, which in the example appears as under $5\frac{1}{2}$ per cent, I should expect to find more common in a larger sample of the population. In the same way, women living in unlegalized unions are generally to be found in good grain-growing areas, and so to be more common in Tangajon territory than on the Upper Veveno. The examples quoted above support this view, as there were 4 in Kavacoc village and only 2 in the three Veveno villages combined.

11. *Divorce*

Divorce, *ariyaan*, is said to be more frequent now than formerly: it may be arranged at the wish of either party, and once the two families have agreed, all the cattle and other gifts exchanged on marriage are returned. The children go with their mother and there are no paternity cases.

VII

THOUGHT AND RELIGION

UNFORTUNATELY, I did not have sufficient time at my disposal to study religion, which is possibly the most complex sphere of Murle life, nor, for such an absorbing and obtruse subject, did I learn the full range of colour terms, which the Murle use to denote, for example, an affinity between objects sharing the same colour conformation that to an outsider is quite obscure. Their colour vocabulary is both extensive and comprehensive, and allows them to describe, for example, a beast in one word, where we should require several sentences or phrases. Thus *regec* illustrates the iridescent sheen on fish scales,[1] and the colours of the rainbow. I therefore consider this chapter to be only a partial account of their thought and religion, and yet an endeavour to shed some light on such a diverse subject.

Inevitable linguistic limitations made it difficult for me to understand the full range of symbolism in Murle thought, and much of the dualism in their philosophy; and the fact that for them words have associations, as well as meanings, proved a constant barrier in trying to unravel 'hard' topics. In the Murle view everything is 'linked together', and all the various strands are so closely interwoven that it is almost impossible to start at the beginning in the study of a particular sphere of their life, and follow it through to its logical conclusion, and all too easy to miss the overtones of a particular definition. I believe, however, from my observations and contacts with the people, that this interweaving of different ideas into a coherent pattern is part of their very texture of thought and expression, particularly in their songs, which are so full of allusion, and association of words and ideas, that a few carefully chosen words naturally convey far more to a fellow tribesman who is well informed about their customs than to a stranger trying to elucidate them. Their songs and sayings, which employ archaic words not understood by ordinary Murle—it was only the *gayok* who could explain them to me, and even then, not always as fully

---

[1] Cf. pp. 129 n., 133.

as I could have wished—are learnt by heart and transmitted from one generation to another, so providing a method of preserving tribal traditions and beliefs, and, in turn, the continuity of their thought. To add to my own linguistic difficulties, my literate Murle assistants were too young, and their knowledge of English too restricted, for them to be of much assistance to me in this connection.

Some of the concepts that help to form the distinctive content of Murle thought have already been discussed; the account of their rain dances and ceremonies of war, in particular, were described in Chapter IV. The part played by the drumchiefs in these ceremonies was so vital that no assessment of their influence and authority could be made without reference to them. It was impossible for me to see a rain dance or a dance of victorious warriors after a raid, for none was held during my tenure of office. As a result, I was only able to record their own descriptions of these ceremonies, which were of outstanding importance in the past, because it was then that the tribe, or large sections of it, prayed to God with the drumchiefs acting as high priests, leading their followers.

The distinction made by us between the supernatural or religious side of life, on the one hand, and the matter-of-fact or secular aspect, on the other, does not exist so clearly for the Murle. They are extremely conscious of the spirit world, and believe that many things which we should ascribe to rational causes are the result of events beyond their control, and have in some unexplained way affected the spirits of their ancestors. For this reason, most personal prayers are directed to the spirits of their ancestors, who, it is hoped, will be in a better position to intercede with God on their behalf. With their conception of the continuity of the family and clan, of the spirits of former members of the tribe, of those living and those yet unborn, this is quite logical; it is a community all of whose members are united in a peculiar way by joint self-interest. The reciprocal obligations involved by this relationship are inescapable for any Murle, and in no sphere of action are they more important than in those where intangible or moral questions are involved. The emphasis on a group-membership is particularly strong in any situation in which the spirit world is, or could conceivably be, involved. It is believed that every human being has a spirit of 'breath' which will persist, on its escaping the confines

of the body after death, to join the ancestral spirits in the underworld. It is also believed that every human being is accompanied,
while on earth, by two guardian birds[1]—one of life and one of
death. Some people, it is thought, have the power of seeing these
birds, and to them they occasionally appear in dreams, to warn of
threatening dangers in the future; more rarely, it is said, they
appear to other people. Giraffe, although commonly hunted, are
thought to be God's creatures, and it is considered dangerous,
when out hunting, to come upon one giving birth. At the beginning
of the rains they are thought to take supernatural flight and dis-
appear into a sudden squall. The Murle do not believe that these
manifestations of the spirit world can ever be wholly comprehen-
sible to mortals, though, of course, some are more gifted than
others in this respect; they are felt to be part of the mystery of life.

It is against this background of belief, in a world not wholly
comprehended, and therefore more to be feared, that their attitude
towards religion must be considered. It explains their interest in
omens, the importance of the mortuary ceremonies, their fear of
witchcraft and the evil eye, and the numerous propitiatory sacrifices that are made at all important events in life, to induce the
help and co-operation of the ancestral spirits.

1. *Attitude towards God*

The immanence of God has already been emphasized, as well
as the significance of Jen, the east and the place of their creation;
thus it is natural for them to oppose Jen with *nyagi*, the west, the
path of the spirits, *gol ci miningit*, where the sun sets. The rainbow
in particular is 'one of God's things', and, according to one of their
myths on the finding of fire, it was the rainbow which first handed
a lighted brand to Dog, who made them combustible (lit. 'gave fire
to the trees'), and brought fire back to man; from then on he was
able to put it to his own uses. Hence, in songs, the sacred fire of
the chiefs is often referred to as the 'fire of the rainbow'. Fire and
water are the two elements used in almost all their ceremonies,
and in Murle eyes both are closely associated with, and thought
to derive from, God, which explains much of the symbolism
inherent in their thought. In a similar manner they consider the
rainbow, the rain serpent, and the python to be closely associated.
'They are all one'—this not implying that they are identical, but

[1] Cf. pp. 78, 136.

that they are linked and share some of the same attributes. The rain serpent, *kutel*, will be discussed later; at this stage it is sufficient to note that they think in this way, identifying, in some contexts, categories of phenomena because of the ideas they suggest.

In this group the python, *uriang*, is clearly recognized as being of less importance than the rain serpent, which, in its turn, is of less significance than the rainbow that is above this world in the sky. In their eyes, all these phenomena are manifestations of God, just as shooting stars and thunderbolts are outward signs of some action by God. Shooting stars, in particular, are believed to be on their way to the sacred drums with important messages, and it is with the ordering of the universe, the changing seasons, and like matters that they consider God is most concerned. Although they assert that he is omnipotent and can be angered by men's doings, they say in contradiction that He is remote and beyond human understanding, and appear to be genuinely unsure how they really regard Him. The following phrases were used to me to describe the way God works: 'He works mysteriously, making things by night; He makes everything, and then kills everything; He makes things, and then breaks them again.'

The greatest importance is attached by the Murle to dreams, and they are often unwilling to discuss them. At the same time they admit that, although many dreams are incomprehensible to ordinary mortals, some people have the power of discerning their portent, while certain seers and soothsayers are greatly venerated for this power. As one old man put it: 'He told them of old in dreams. He told them He made everything to be animal or human, working in the dark of night. It was our ancestors who came down from heaven and saw God who told us that He was short like a spirit and covered all over with long hair.' I was generally told that God 'is like a very small man covered with long hair; his colour is ugly, *cankac*, like a man working: his skin is not like ours, it is grey, *gidang*'. A similar belief is reported from the Turkana.[1] In contradiction, other informants told me that God was immensely tall, that He possessed all the colours of the rainbow, and that His colour term was *regec*.[2] God usually clothes Himself in the angry

[1] '. . . The deity whose appearance is that of a man wearing a complete suit of baboon hair', E. W. Emley, *Man*, 113 (August 1930).

[2] This may account for the erstwhile prohibition against eating fish, which still exists for the Didinga, for it would be considered as partaking of some of the supernatural qualities of the rainbow (cf. p. 126).

grey of dark thunder clouds, implying obscurity and inscrutability, although in His omnipotence He could manifest Himself in any colour he chose.

When I inquired into the prohibition against eating fish, the invariable reply was '*Gi ci Tammu nen*', 'they are God's things', and no reason could be advanced for the fact that they are now eaten in abundance. Driberg, writing of the Didinga, says that 'they speak of fish as the spirits of the river or *borogich ci kido*', and comments that *borogech* is one of the names for the rainbow',[1] which tends to confirm the identification of the rain with God. To the Murle the word *kido* implies one particular river, the 'little rainbows of the sacred river of Jen, the place of creation', whereas to the Didinga it appears to mean any river.

Another question which none of my informants could elucidate was the connection between *kido*, the sacred river or Jen, *kidong*, the drum, *kidoyi*, the mists around the mountain tops at dawn, and *kidori*, the special pieces of meat set aside for the ancestors when any sacrifice is made. All the old men with whom I discussed this were aware of the connection, but unable to give an explanation. Some of them pointed out that *kidoyi* were regarded as particularly significant manifestations of divine power, and the fact that the mountains round Boma are often obscured by morning mists during the rains may be one of the reasons they regard all mountains—even the two little hills, Lothir and Lokicar, in Lotilla —as being awesome mysterious places where unexplained fires are sometimes seen; these are usually ascribed to rain serpents which are thought to frequent caves and crannies in rocky mountains, and it is possibly significant that the sacred drums were often kept in mountain caves. Whether these emotions are induced in the Murle because mountains are high, and consequently nearer to God (in their concept of space), or because of the universal awe that the grandeur and remoteness of high places enveloped by swirling rain clouds inspire, I could not deduce. Indeed, it was almost impossible to analyse their thoughts on God, the rain, and the mountains, and I am inclined to think that this was partly due to the fact that they were not very sure themselves. While they consider it the duty of an individual to fear and respect God, they find it difficult to explain exactly what this entails, beyond observing the tribal

---

[1] J. H. Driberg, 'A Preliminary Account of the Didinga', *Sudan Notes and Records*, vol. v (1922).

virtues of courage, fair dealings, generosity, and, of course, respect for the customs of their tribe.

2. *Celestial Attitudes*

The space between the sky above and the earth beneath is thought to be filled by the wind. As clouds and storms can be seen to move across the sky, behind it is regarded as Tammu's sphere of action. Above the clouds the sun, moon, and stars are thought to move across the surface of the sky at His direction. Although I was told there were a few Murle with expert knowledge of the stars— and it would be surprising if such an observant people had no such experts—I never met one. Most people knew a few of the commoner constellations, the myths about the moon and sun, and something of the Maindherbo stories—I say stories advisedly, because I was told there were many of them—but I found it difficult to piece them together, although every child knows that the Pleiades are the children of a former Murle chief named Maindherbo, and a few lines of the relevant song. According to one version, Maindherbo was the first man sent down from heaven with his wife to people the earth. In due course his wife bore him eight sons and eight daughters at a single birth, and a year later repeated the performance. As they grew up the boys ganged together and went their own way, leaving the girls at home. But one day the two parties met out in the bush and paired off, the girls being very intrigued with the boys' tails, with which they could not resist playing. Eventually they made the boys lie down, sat on top of them, and put the tails into their *kabongkarota*; the boys enjoyed this, and ever after made the girls lie down, and lay on top of them. In due course the girls bore children, and the families scattered to become the ancestors of the various tribes on earth. This version of the creation is far less common than that of the 'rib' given on page 20, although 'Are you Maindherbo?' *niina ein(?) Maindherbo*, a remark frequently made to anyone pretending to be a know-all, suggests that Maindherbo has his own place in their mythology.

The tale of Maindherbo's death in old age is much commoner: by then he had grown so fat, living on milk from his innumerable herds, that he could no longer walk, but had to stay at home, while his wives and children went out to work in the fields or herd his cattle. One day, when they had left him at home as usual, a party of dwarfs, *cilicel*, arrived with their hunting dogs; Maindherbo, unable to defend himself, was killed, cut up, and eaten. In the evening, when his wives and unmarried daughters returned, they found the invaders gorged with meat and asleep by the hut. Quietly, without waking them, dwarfs and dogs were put inside the hut and burnt to death; and Maindherbo's remaining daughters were so overcome with grief that they left this earth and returned to heaven, to become the Pleiades.

When *cilicel* are mentioned the Murle often say: 'Like the *Nyamnyam*', a common term in the Southern Sudan for the Azande, who are popularly supposed to have been cannibals, so that this story may have a historical basis and refer to an ancient incident between the Murle and some Bantu tribe. Whatever the truth of this, the Pleiades appear to be the most significant constellation in the sky for the Murle, and it is certain that Maindherbo is connected with peopling the earth.

The Great Bear and the Little Bear were also recognized, the former being the 'commoner's elephant'; the three stars forming the handle of the Plough are the owners of the first and second spears (in consequence they claim special rights), and of the stone on which the hunters' spears are sharpened, *et ci beo*; the Little Bear is the 'chiefs' elephant'. Apart from *Dumec* — which I failed to identify—this appears to be the limit of the ordinary man's identification of stars.

The connecting link between the sky (or heaven), the wind (or atmosphere), and the earth is in some sense the rainbow, and, of course, its attendants—the closely related rain serpent and the ill-omened python. The importance of the rainbow, its obvious connection with rain, and its believed connection with the origin of fire in Murle mythology, are sufficient to give it a key position in the thought and imagery of a people who use the same word for sky, rain, and God. In some sense it is a visible projection of the Supreme Being from His place on high to the earth below, only seen when He is beneficently watering the earth with rain. For rain is thought to be 'good', as opposed to thunder which is 'bad', or at least potentially dangerous, and is sometimes called the 'roaring of the rainbow', whose powers are in some sense thought to be shared by the rain serpent and python. Here again they are regarded as 'one', although not identical. In practice little attention is paid to pythons, which are not common, although to come across one curled up asleep is considered dangerous, and probably a warning that disaster will overcome the traveller or his family. To meet a python on the move is worse still, and thought to presage a death in the family, or to the individual concerned.

3. *The Rain Serpents*

Kutel, the rain serpents, on the other hand, are considered so sinister that the people do not care to discuss them: they are too closely related to the manifestations of God's power in thunder and lightning, despite the fact that the frequent and violent thunderstorms of the early rains are welcomed for the crops and grazing land. Still, the accompanying thunder is feared, for it may mean that God is angry. These serpents are described as being enormously long, like an immense python, with a body as thick as a human being. They are said to be red *meirik*, iridescent,[1] and to live only in mountains, spending the daytime in dark recesses of their caves and emerging in the hours of darkness. They are supposed to have two breasts like a woman, with which they suckle their young, although they are supposed to lay eggs as a snake, and have on their heads two tufts or plumes of feathers resembling horns, and at the end of their tails a great claw. They eat birds, small vermin, and insects, foraging at night; they are then said to emit a 'fire-like' substance from their bellies which attracts insects in the darkness, and when sated to swallow the fire.

It is believed that any human being, or even a large animal, seen by a rain serpent would surely die, although, owing to their nocturnal habits and mountainous domain, this rarely happens, and human beings generally detect their gleaming light and make good their escape before being seen by the dreaded monster. Even to have seen one is extremely dangerous, and the story is told of a young man who came back to his village in the Maruwa hills and reported that he had come upon a dead serpent while out hunting: nobody was surprised when he died the following day. The two small rocky outcrops, Lothir and Lokicar, some of the peaks on Boma and amongst the Maruwa hills, as well as Mount Kathiangor, are said to 'have fire', a euphemistic way of saying they are the habitat of rain serpents. All inexplicable fires at night are ascribed to them, and even the steam rising from the ground after a shower at the end of the hot weather is said to be caused by them.

[1] Cf. pp. 126, 129 n. 2.

Women pray to them, as to the drums, to intercede with God on their behalf to grant them children.

4. *Death and the After-life*

The universe they consider to be round and flat, although it has four corners or horns where 'the sky puts down its feet to the earth'. The sky is thought of as inverted downwards 'like a hut'. and there is a similar dome beneath the earth which is the under-world of the spirits, *lok*, a word ordinarily used for a hole in the ground, a pit.

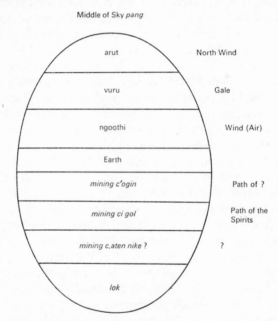

Middle of Sky *pang*

arut — North Wind

vuru — Gale

ngoothi — Wind (Air)

Earth

mining c'ogin — Path of ?

mining ci gol — Path of the Spirits

mining c,aten nike ? — ?

lok

There are said to be various entrances to the underworld, the best known being at *Gerok*, a lake in the Maruwa hills, where the lowing of departed cattle is said to be heard when the waters of the lake are particularly low. It is to this underworld that the spirits go after death, 'walking on one leg', and gradually becoming smaller and smaller with the passing of time; the spirits of their cattle are also supposed to join their ancestors. Although spirits can return to the earth by night, and sometimes do so to trouble their descendants, they must return to the underworld before dawn.

The practice of removing the two central incisors from the lower jaw, observed by all Murle, is explained by the necessity of allowing a person's soul to escape from his body at death. If, as sometimes happens in old age, the teeth have grown together, two more are supposed to be broken after death, to ensure a safe passage to the underworld for the spirit of the deceased. This should be done by the undertaker, *ngambi*, if one is available, but if it is feared that he will not come quickly, any other person present who is not related to the family may be asked to perform this rite. *Ngambi* are a class of people, usually poor, who carry out the duties of the mortuary rites for a small fee, and on the occurrence of death in a homestead one is sent for immediately.

The corpse is normally exposed in the bush to the west of the village in the afternoon, perhaps half a mile or so away. It is carried on a sleeping-skin, usually by neighbours. No member of the homestead in which the death occurred may eat or drink until the vultures have started to devour the corpse. If death occurs during the night, the corpse is carried out of the hut without delay, and a special fire is lit, as it is considered unlucky for any one who might subsequently use the hut if the corpse remains inside for any length of time. If the head of a homestead falls ill and is expected to die, he should go and live in the hut of his senior wife, as it is her right and duty to carry his head when he is lifted out of the hut for the last time: his body will be laid, for a short interval, in a place where the cattle can see it, so that they too may know that their master is dead.

When the undertaker arrives he takes all the food already prepared in the homestead, as it is thought to be dangerous for relatives of the deceased; he also takes the personal trinkets, ornaments, weapons, skins, tobacco pouches, and other of his belongings, leaving only the family armpit cowbell, a special spear or so, and the sacred firesticks, which are inherited by the eldest son. He then sweeps out the hut and shaves the heads of all relatives present, who remove their bracelets, rings, and other ornaments—which should be laid aside for the best part of a year—as the outward signs of mourning. In the afternoon the undertaker leads all the relatives down to the river or nearest pool, where they bathe, the undertaker washing each one individually. This may be a perfunctory gesture, in which he sprinkles a little water on each member of the party—the import is symbolical rather than factual

—having the significance of a ritual purification by water from the ill effects of death.

The party then returns to the homestead and the undertaker lights a new fire, on which special plants are burnt to purify the hut: he waves the smoke over each relative and beats them all with a bunch of the plants. On the completion of purification by water and fire the ceremonies are at an end for the day, although the undertaker will probably return in two or three days' time to ensure that his task has been properly completed; and if any close relatives have arrived he will repeat the ceremony with them to ward off any ill effects. With this, the first part of the rites is complete. Three to six months later, or even longer, a second ceremony is held, which is thought to be of far greater significance —the disposal of the spirit, as opposed to the body. The Murle say that undertakers 'take away' or 'cleanse' the spirit and the birds,[1] *aara miningit aara hibaalic.* The same undertaker may be employed for this ceremony, or, if the family is wealthy, a noted doctor may be asked to perform the rite, the undertaker acting as his assistant. It is considered important that all close relatives of the deceased should be present, particularly if they were absent at the previous ceremony. The doctor, or his assistant, carefully questions all present about the wishes of the deceased, for it is thought that, if these are faithfully carried out, the spirit will go swiftly and happily to join its relatives in the underworld, without troubling those still alive, causing them sickness, appearing in dreams, or haunting the homestead in efforts to force them to carry out its wishes. Thus it is felt to be spiritually dangerous for relatives to neglect the last wishes of a dying person, and if an owl or other bird should settle on one of the huts of the homestead in the evening, the relatives will scare it away with lighted brands and then consult a diviner as to the cause of the visitation.

The outward form of this removal or disposal of the spirit is expressed by the relatives sitting down on the ground every evening for a week or so, while the undertaker or doctor chants songs. The relatives, arranged in a rough semicircle, beat time on the ground in front of them with their sandals and join in the chorus. In between songs the undertaker addresses them, exhorting them repeatedly to tell him all the wishes of the deceased, so that they may be carried out and thus expedite the departure of a

[1] Cf. pp. 78, 128.

contented spirit to the underworld. At other times the undertaker addresses the spirit, recounting the wishes that have been complied with, promising that others will be dealt with, and assuring it that there is no reason for its return to the earth by night to haunt the homestead.

If a man is killed fighting, dies a violent death out hunting, or is drowned, the preliminary rites for the disposal of the body do not necessitate the services of a doctor, although in these circumstances it is all the more difficult for a spirit and his attendant birds to be safely guided to the underworld. If foul play is suspected, it is the duty of the senior wife to keep one or two of his bones, sometimes for years, so that at some time in the future, perhaps when a son has grown up, the death may be avenged. The bones are carefully sewn in a skin for their protection, and sometimes placed in the nearest pool, for it is believed that it is fatal for people with 'blood between them' to drink out of the same gourd. So strong is this belief that it is thought that, if a killer were to drink water from the same part of the river as that concealing the bones, his evil deeds would be avenged upon him.

To their Nuer and Anuak neighbours the Murle preoccupation with the spiritual dangers of death appears paradoxical, in the light of what they consider the Murle's impious and incorrect custom of exposing their dead to be eaten by vultures and hyenas. The strength of these convictions, however, and their diligence in ensuring a happy and peaceful departure of the spirit, are such that the subsequent social behaviour of the relatives is strongly influenced by them.

5. *Categories of Witch Doctor*

In all the mystery surrounding rain serpents, their most significant attribute for the Murle is their possession of the *kwolo*, mythical insects—'like bees but only the size of mosquitoes' I was told—which all diviners and soothsayers are supposed, in turn, to have in their heads, and whose possession gives them their special powers in interpreting the future, diagnosing illness, averting evil and misfortune, and eradicating uncleanness. In Murle thought the diviners' unusual powers are linked to the rain serpent, from which the *kwolo* they possess are derived, then to the rainbow, and so to the omnipotent Tammu and his manifestation in the rainbow. This is their explanation of, and, in a sense, the derivation of, the special powers of these doctors, *ngarec*, who, although normal human beings, nevertheless possess supranormal powers, are something more than human in the ordinary sense of the term, and play a very significant role in everyday life. *Anyak kwolo*: 'They have—or possess—these supernatural insects in their heads.' I had heard of doctors and their *kwolo* some time before rain serpents, and when I asked whence they came, was told: 'From Tammu'; and it was only during subsequent investigations that I realized the inference that they came from the rain serpents, and that this was a particular link with the Supreme Being.

There are four kinds of *ngarrec*: *ngarrec ci caava*, sandal thrower, who is consulted before a journey is undertaken; the pebble diviner, *ngarrec ci kagura*, far less common and thought to be able to foretell events in the distant future; fire doctors, *ngarrec ci goyo*, the most numerous and more than half of them women, who profess to cure innumerable aches and pains; and *ngarrec ci koloktecu*, augurs or seers, who foretell the future by reading the omens revealed to them from the intestines of sacrificial animals.

Although working in different fields, all must be taught by a practitioner who is already an expert in his own craft, and acquire their knowledge mainly by assisting their instructor; but the crucial part is the gradual introduction of *kwolo* into the learner's head. This process is thought to be extremely dangerous, because to be possessed by *kwolo* without the necessary knowledge of how to control them can drive people mad or even to destroy themselves. A doctor is therefore said to administer *kwolo* to his pupil by degrees, and only when he is satisfied that the learner will be in command of them. If a pupil acquires more *kwolo* than he can control, a special plant, *karadaic*, is burnt as an offering to the rain serpent, but even if this rite is performed, I was told, it is not always sufficient to prevent unfortunate results; and considerable emphasis is laid on the point that although *ngarrecs'* powers can, and should, be used for good, their abuse is fraught with danger, which also applies to the powers of chiefs through their possession of the sacred drums. The most obvious difference in the nature of the powers of doctors possessed of *kwolo* is that they normally use them for the benefit of individuals who consult them on personal matters, whereas the chiefs' powers are used for the benefit of the whole community; and it is the fact that they are so concerned with witchcraft and the evil eye that raises the part played by doctors to such importance in society. Almost all misfortunes and ailments are ascribed to the machinations of some malevolent neighbour or ill-wisher, and naturally witchcraft is not an easy subject to discuss with the Murle: it is too full of evil implication and too near at hand for anybody to speak of it freely.

Although they know and can recognize the symptoms of a number of illnesses, the border line between (what we should regard as) physical ailment and pure mischance is not so clearly defined for them. If someone slips and falls, hurting his foot or ankle in the process, we are inclined to think him either clumsy or unlucky: both of these possibilities occur to the Murle, but there is also suspicion that magic has played a part in the mishap—'Why slip at that particular place in those particular circumstances?' they would ask, and although the former causes are not ruled out, the fear persists of malevolence on the part of some person possessing magical powers, enabling him to use the victim's clumsiness to harm him. Thus it is thought advisable to consult a diviner before setting off on a journey, or contemplating any serious undertaking, to ensure that the occasion is in every way propitious. Again, while some illnesses are accepted fatalistically as the will of God, *dhodh ci Tammu nen*, others at once arouse suspicions of witchcraft. *Ngarrec* are therefore dealing with matters on two planes; the physical, where particular plants are believed to afford relief, and of which the doctors are supposed to have special knowledge, and the spiritual or psychological plane, where their supranormal powers are believed to be able to assist in warding off or averting evil influences.

The sandal diviners are most common, because nearly all Murle know something of their art. Briefly, the procedure consists of taking a pair of sandals, putting them sole to sole, and holding them by the heels. They are then tapped two or three times on the ground and tossed quite gently into the air. This is repeated several times, and the art is to be able to read the answer revealed by the pattern in which they fall. I frequently watched sandals thrown, and, although the patterns and their numerous combinations were explained to me on each occasion, I was an insufficiently adept pupil to understand their meaning. Good diviners are thought to be able to foretell events for the following few days with considerable accuracy, and inevitably their reputations and the respect accorded to them vary according to the success of their forecasts.

Pebble divining is a much more highly prized accomplishment: not only are the *ngarrec ci kagura* thought to be able to foretell events in the more distant future, but their predictions are considered more accurate and reliable. Tambarun, a leading expert in this field, threw the pebbles for me several times, and the method he used corresponded almost exactly with that described by Driberg amongst the Didinga.[1] Forty-eight pebbles are employed and kept in a special pouch when not in use. The diviner generally asks for a sleeping-skin on which to throw the pebbles, and, according to Tambarun, the more intimately this skin is connected with the questioner, the better will be the result. For much the same reason it was his custom to ask the questioner to hold the pebbles in his hands, breathe on them, put them against his head, and so on, so that the pebbles should get to know the questioner. These preliminaries took some time; when they were completed, Tambarum picked up a handful of pebbles, shook them in his hands for a few seconds, and then threw them gently on to the ground in front of him. Immediately he started subtracting four at a time, until less than four were left. This number was scored and the process repeated. Once the remainder was four—or nothing—the first line was completed and he started scoring a second, and so on. If the first quota of answers, given after using up all the forty-eight pebbles, was incomplete, he started all over again, and he told me that it was sometimes necessary to do this repeatedly. The art of the diviner consists of knowing how to read the resulting rows of figures. In my own case what he told me was subsequently proved correct, although, as a foreigner with a very distant homeland, I was considered a very difficult subject; and this fact suitably enhanced his established reputation. Although he usually charged a sheep or goat for his services, my consultation fee was paid in tobacco.

In a tribe where physical sickness is so prevalent, and where the fear of malevolent influences is so acute, it is not surprising that fire doctors practice their art more frequently than do any of the others: almost every evening one can hear the singing which accompanies their rites from a near-by homestead. The songs are full of topical allusions and are clearly one of the means by which news of events is circulated. Indeed, I was told that at these sessions —which always take place after dark—news was broadcast even

[1] J. H. Driberg, 'Divination by Pebbles', *Man*, 3 (1933).

more than at the midday meetings of elders at the clubs, where it is inevitably discussed. Sometimes fire doctors work in pairs, or even in groups of three or four, although one doctor is generally in charge, assisted by two or three apprentices to whom he is teaching the art. There are usually several patients sitting on skins on one side of a wood fire, with the doctor and his assistants on the other. He leads the singing, the rest joining in the chorus, a practice which I was told was necessary to generate a feeling of confidence and good fellowship. From time to time a patient is asked to explain his symptoms, and very often to indicate who he thinks has caused them. There may well be some benefit for the patient in a friendly atmosphere engendered by songs and jokes, and the morbid fear of spells cast may well be eased by confession and sharing the burden with one trained to dissipate evil.

The Murle suffer frequent rheumatic aches and pains, and from time to time during these nocturnal meetings their limbs and joints are massaged by the doctors and assistants, sometimes gently, at other times violently, their limbs being flexed, patted, and occasionally thumped with force. The climax is usually the 'production' of a piece of stick or stone from the injured part of the patient's body by the doctor-in-chief; this is greeted by grunts of surprise and awe, although nobody could really be surprised at such a frequent occurrence. Sessions last for some hours, from about 8.00 p.m. until midnight or later, and many people told me they felt better afterwards, although the results were only temporary, and, of course, necessitated their return for repeated treatment.

There are few *ngarrec ci koloktecu*, but those who follow this calling are greatly respected. They are not often consulted by individuals, although no major tribal venture would be undertaken without their reading the omens, which they do by examining the intestines of a sheep or goat sacrificed for the purpose. Their pronouncements are expressed in such cryptic terms as a rule that no one is quite sure of their meaning until after the event. In 1943 Tori, the most noted seer at the time, announced that there was a great danger of sickness sweeping the country and that therefore no dances should be held. Although his warning was exceedingly unpopular, and not obeyed literally, indeed he had no power to ban dances, they were restricted that year for fear of invoking the sickness he had foretold. Another year he gave a more specific warning that there would be good rains right at the beginning of the wet season, that those who succeeded in establishing their crops early would reap a good harvest, but that those who delayed would have poor crops: to the benefit of his prestige, events turned out as he had predicted.

The Murle undoubtedly feel a need for the services of these augurs to ward off the evil influences in the world around them, whether they are due to witchcraft, their unquiet ancestors, or just mischance; and although they are valued for the help they give, it is fully realized that any assistance is limited in its efficacy. There is general fear of the unseen forces which shape men's lives, and of the misfortunes which afflict mortals on this earth, and it is consistent with this attitude that the greatest moral indignation should be engendered by witchcraft, incest, and killing a fellow tribesman by steel, because these offences are felt to be spiritually dangerous for the community as a whole, as well as transgressing against their individual victims.

6. *Witches and Witchcraft*

The fear of witchcraft, *tamaar*, is widespread, and the subject much discussed in a furtive manner. To broach the subject openly might be to invite reprisals, so that to find out if there is witchcraft in a village one asks if there is 'whispering', *ngumtin*: to accuse anyone directly of being a witch, *tamarac*, is courting danger, because the accusation, if proved, carries the death penalty. I knew of several homesteads 'with whispering', and was advised to brush my hand across my face to avert any ill effects when talking with a suspected witch. It is thought that witches and wizards are poisoners, obtaining special roots and plants from Boma, and beyond in Ethiopia, with which they make concoctions to put in the food of their victims. But the most insidious poison of all— believed to be fatal—is made by obtaining a piece of human flesh, and grinding it to powder; in a community where corpses are exposed this presents small likelihood of detection. In the past, if a man caught a witch trying to damage his crops, he would attack him with a stick until the witch cried for mercy, and was prepared to ransom himself with a bracelet or similar object, which would be stored away carefully and produced as evidence later if the evil-doer continued his nefarious practices.

Witches were only brought to trial if someone became seriously ill, ascribed his sickness to witchcraft, and made a formal accusation at the village club, but if sufficient evidence could be produced by other homesteads the witch would be forced to admit his guilt. Once the feelings of the community were sufficiently outraged, the penalty was execution, *marinet ci tameracu*, 'the begging of the witch', by the mob, *kolla*; at a pre-arranged time the men of the afflicted village repaired to the offender's homestead and beat him to death with sticks, snapped off nearby trees or bushes specially for the occasion, which were afterwards thrown on top of the corpse, one being inserted in the anus 'to see that he died quickly'. A few cases of this occurrence during the past twenty years were quoted to me; the most notorious being that of Oleo, who was killed in this manner Toddoi on the Upper Lotilla in 1932.

> Arui alaan Gaaga!
> Arui alaan Gaaga!
> Ma owudi Maimjim
> Kawudi lauaarec elle
>
> Kukucol Kenga
> Kakadawa dherwa
> Baladomah ligonya.

In rough translation:

> He beat a chief for nothing!
> He beat a chief for nothing!
> If you drank of the water of Maimjim
> Your arms would smart
>   and your stomach be ruptured
> But now the vultures
> Have eaten him and his village is deserted.

I was always told that it was the fear of calamity befalling the community as a result of such unnatural and anti-social behaviour, rather than the offences themselves, that worried people.

Another deep-seated fear of witches was due to the belief that they were so depraved as to break the prohibition against using steel on a fellow tribesman; most of them were expected to desist from their evil practices after a few severe drubbings, but there remained the fear that, if cornered, a witch might ensure his finder's silence by spearing him to death. 'Blood is bad', *biyei gerdhe*, they said so often; meaning that it was spiritually dangerous to the community as a whole, as well as to those who shed it; it was for that reason that witches were beaten to death, and those guilty of *ngilidh*—a term perhaps best translated as incest, but which included all forms of sexual perversion—were hanged (if possible, no blood was shed at their execution).

7. The Evil Eye

Although the evil eye is considered to be as prevalent as witchcraft, it is discussed less. There are two words to express it, *ralinet* and *pelanin*, and although they really mean the same thing, the second is considered the safer word to use in ordinary conversation because it names a milder version of the same power. A man possessing *pelanin* can cause the sickness of a child or calf, but not its death, whereas the possessor of *ralinet* is believed to be able to cause the death of a grown person. The Murle say that the possessor of this power looks out of the corner of his eyes, and has colours in them which are dangerous. The word used for 'colour', *bayen*, in this connection is the same as that used for the colour conformation of cattle.

It is thought that in some way these colours are able to send pieces of grass or mud from the eyes of the possessor of the evil eye to the *legerwac*, the large intestine in his victim's stomach. These foreign bodies 'tear' the intestine, thus causing sickness or death. Anyone with a pain in his stomach, therefore, consults a doctor without delay. The latter is usually able to diagnose his patient's condition from his symptoms, and it is said that a person suffering from the effects of the evil eye cannot eat properly. The doctor tries to remove *aara*, the grass or lump of mud, from the patient's intestine by massage with hot wood ashes, but if there is any doubt about the diagnosis a lamb or kid is sacrificed as part of the cure. If, when the entrails of the beast are examined, any foreign body, such as a ball of hair, a stick, or a fruit stone, is found in them, it is considered conclusive proof that the patient is suffering from the evil eye, and he and his relatives will then cast about to discover who is the instigator.

So dangerous are the powers of the possessor of the evil eye believed to be that he has to take special precautions with his own children and with the offspring of his flocks and herds. When his wife bears him a child he is said to close his eyes before approaching it, take the child's fists and put them against his closed eyes, and open the child's mouth and spit into it, in order to ensure that no ill effects should inadvertently befall it. Much the same procedure is followed with calves and kids, as it is particularly the young, whether human or animal, that are thought to be likely to suffer. Many good-natured persons who have inherited these evil powers warn their neighbours of the possible danger, and perform the same ritual with their children and calves to prevent untoward effects.

8. *Theft and Compensation*

Theft is recognized to be a serious offence against the community, as well as against the individual. A man of the Nyilim age-set, for instance, who had previously been stealing animals from neighbouring villages, was done to death at Ngarwaalin during the early rains of 1935 for stealing a ram: this was considered and execution, *kamaar*, justified because the people of the neighbourhood would no longer tolerate his continued delinquency. At much the same time Abokiri, a Tapotha who was living at Mainyurany village, stole a sheep, which he cooked and ate in his field. Because he was a foreigner and a guest he was not executed but soundly beaten with sandals, tied up, and taken to his host, who had to pay a sheep in compensation.

Normally the punishment for theft is not heavy; the stolen articles must be restored to their owner, or compensation paid in lieu, with possibly a sheep or goat in atonement, depending on the circumstances of the particular offence. Theft of cattle is practically unknown because nobody could hope to get away with it. The seizure of cattle by force in settlement of a debt is not regarded as theft, but is resorted to as a means of securing the repayment, and any resort to violence in such cases is regarded as a legitimate expedient to bring the dispute to the notice of the elders and ensure that it will be settled by them.

For a party of young men to kill an ox for food when hungry, without first asking the owner's consent, is regarded as a form of begging, *marinet*, and incurs a debt for which one of the party will have to make future settlement by paying a cow calf. If a young man runs up to an ox after a dance, or at Mowi,[1] and spears it, without asking the owner's permission, it is known as *taraar*. The culprit is liable to pay the recognized compensation, but it is a

[1] Cf. p. 91.

socially accepted form of behaviour and not theft, because there are witnesses present and the killer knows the resultant liability to be his. On the other hand, for a man to kill an ox or sheep when alone and without witnesses is a very dangerous act, because, although he might plead it was *taraar*, or that he was dying of hunger, he would be strongly suspected of being a thief or of seeking to avoid the liability incurred, which amounts to much the same thing.

Liben, housebreaking, and destroying a grain store, *oyok pem*, are both serious offences, but 'borrowing' a personal possession such as a spear or dance ornament without the owner's permission, although it may give rise to ill feeling, is not regarded as a crime against the community. Stealing a few head of new grain from the standing crops does not, as a rule, involve the payment of compensation: 'He was hungry', they say, but the relations of a lad who did so repeatedly in 1949 were fined a sheep.

Real theft, which is done furtively and with the deliberate intent of avoiding the liability incurred, is regarded with the utmost scorn; but the gradation from this to forced loans without the owner's consent, and to the 'borrowing' of an article without permission, both of which may cause considerable annoyance at the time, provides a wide field for discussion at the clubs, where these disputes are settled. Provided the liability is admitted and the need can be shown to have been genuine or urgent, an individual is permitted by custom to take what he requires for a particular purpose, and repay it or make good the loss to the owner in the future. There is a regular and well-known scale of compensation of payments, so that the taker knows the liability he is incurring. Rich men are often not averse to being owed many debts, because, while cattle may die from a variety of natural causes, a debt can only be cancelled by the payment of the prescribed compensation.

Loans, whether voluntary or socially recognized forms of forced loan, provide the only method open to the Murle of banking surplus stock, and in practice play a considerable part in the Murle economy.

There is, therefore, a close relationship between the compensation equivalents—for example, a cow calf for an ox—which comes into play when (1) a loan is made and the borrower incurs the liability of repaying its equivalent in the future; (2) a forced loan is imposed, the owner is not consulted, but the borrower's liability is admitted; and (3) it is a theft, where the thief tries to avoid admitting liability by leaving no trace. In all cases compensation must be paid, assuming the thief is caught, and a complicated scale of equivalents, built up from many precedents, exists for this part of the settlement. If the owner was caused considerable loss or inconvenience when the loan was forced on him, atonement too may be demanded, and is often awarded. A thief may have to atone for his sins with a beating, or, as a last resort, with his life, because an example must be made for the sake of maintaining the standards of morality in the tribe.

9. *Insult*

Insulting remarks or behaviour, *dominet*, are regarded as very serious offences, and heavy penalties are often imposed by the elders for any such breach of good manners. Whether or not a particular remark is regarded as an insult depends entirely on the relative position in the social structure of the two persons concerned. The grossest insults are commonly exchanged between members of the same age-set and treated as jokes, whereas an insulting remark addressed by a young man to an elder would be severely punished; the young man would certainly be made to pay a sheep or goat as atonement to the elders, and possibly compensation to the man he had insulted as well.

To call another person a wizard is also dangerous, because the accusation, if unrebutted, carries dangerous penalties for the accused; here again the social status of the persons concerned plays a large part in assessing the seriousness of the offence.

10. *Cursing*

One of the strongest sanctions operating in society is that afforded by cursing, *torin*. A kinsman who thinks that he has not been given his fair share of the distribution of marriage cattle will not hesitate to bring pressure to bear on the bride's parents by cursing them. An adulterer, who has been punished for his offence, will resort to the same expedient if he considers his punishment too severe. Cursing is greatly feared, because it is thought that some sickness will result, or that a kinswoman will be rendered barren thereby. It is most efficacious within a kinship group, because it is thought that the ancestral spirits will be annoyed and want the wrong which caused it remedied. In particular, it provides a safeguard for members of a kinship group who are in a position of juniority against any attempt by those members of the group in a position of seniority to abuse their position at the expense of their juniors. The kinship system attaches so much importance to primogeniture and seniority that this ceremonial cursing may be said to provide a necessary restraint on the misuse of the associated powers, thus ensuring justice within family and kinship groups.

11. *Habitual Offenders*

A few offences were tolerated, compensation and the payment of the 'cow of atonement', *tang ci dilento*, being enforced; but, in the interests of tribal discipline and the continued existence and well-being of the community as a whole, habitual offenders could not be tolerated, because they were spiritually, rather than criminally, dangerous. Eventually their kinsmen felt unable to afford them their protection; the resulting executions were clearly an embryonic form of state rather than lynch law, which is an expression of outraged public opinion in the heat of the moment, while Murle executions were generally performed more in sorrow than anger. Indeed, their reluctance to demand the death penalty illustrates an overriding principle, the freedom of the individual to do as he wishes. In the sphere of individual behaviour they are remarkably free, with the proviso that nothing is done to endanger their collective interests. It is for this reason that so much time is devoted to the settlement of important cases: each one is judged on its own merits, but as one of a series, the amount of provocation and every detail of the relevant circumstances being keenly probed. Nevertheless, persistent flouting of authority and *ker ci Murlu* necessitated severe penalties, and even in *ruwen dilawa*[1] there exists a set procedure for the defence of the offender.

12. *Ownership and Property*

As already stated, in the Murle conception of property the 'land belongs to the chiefs', a particular pool to a particular clan, together with the grazing rights that go with it, cultivation rights to the descendants of the first occupier of the particular area in question, cattle to the head of a family group, and weapons and ornaments to an individual. It is, however, only the personal possessions of an individual which are completely under his control,

[1] Cf. p. 81.

to dispose of as he pleases. Cattle are normally owned by a family, although those bought for tobacco, sheep, or goats, or even grain, may be said to be the property of their owner because he has earned them. In the past cattle captured in war were particularly valuable, because they were not liable to be returned if a kinsman was divorced. These were known as 'cattle of the foot', *ten ci dhocu*, and the same term is applied nowadays to cattle bought from the Government for money. The obligations of kinship, however, may at any time require their surrender to meet some need of the group, or to settle some obligation it incurred in the past. A rich man cannot protest beyond a certain point when a young warrior spears one of his bulls, because it is his turn to provide meat for the dancers and at that particular moment he does not possess a suitable bull.

Ownership of a pool does not give the owner the right to refuse permission to other people to fish therein, only to ensure that they do not fish there before the appropriate sacrifice has been made to the spirit guardian of the pool. Its owner is justified in claiming compensation from anybody fishing there before the appropriate ceremonies have been held, because to do so is an offence against the community as a whole: the guardian spirits would be annoyed, thus endangering the community's food supply. The owner of a pool is the representative, probably because he is the direct descendant of the family group which first captured the pool, but his ownership, though very real in Murle eyes, is strictly limited and includes certain obligations.

In short, the Murle conception of property takes into account the fact that an individual cannot live alone, but only as a member of a community. Kinship obligations provide a form of social security and insurance, and preclude exclusive rights of property for an individual within the kinship group. At the same time, the system of loans and debts which provides for a socially approved form of almost forced loans, prevents the completely exclusive ownership of property by a kinship group within the community as a whole.

With this important provision in mind, it is possible to consider their conception of cattle ownership, their real wealth, and inheritance. As the ownership of cattle is closely linked with kinship obligations, the Murle always speak of cattle as being owned by the head of the *korok*. In practice they are always divided up amongst the various households comprising this unit, and there is therefore little ground for disputes when the head of the *korok* dies. A man's heirs are his sons, and, in particular, the eldest son by his senior wife, who inherits the headship of the *korok*. He disposes of the group's cattle as his father did before him, and is responsible for the settlement of any debts his father may have incurred. The dead man's personal possessions are given away to the *ngambi*, except for his ceremonial armpit cowbell, and, possibly, special spears which are inherited by his eldest son. In practice, certain cattle are given to particular individuals, and the gift is not normally revoked unless a divorce or some offence committed by a member of the *korok* necessitates cattle being paid away. For example, a son should be given his name ox and a heifer to 'start his own herd' when he reaches manhood. A woman can own cattle and receives them when her own daughters and nieces are married; these are inherited by her sons on her death.

If a man or a woman dies without any direct heirs, the property is divided amongst the close relatives, brothers, sisters, and cousins, in the order father's brother's sons, father's sister's sons, mother's brother's sons. Some of the most involved disputes occur when a man dies leaving a very young son whose inheritance is entrusted to a guardian during his minority, and the heir accuses him of misappropriation when he grows up.

13. *Symbols of Unity*

Another important principle in Murle thought is their theory of balance, *venon*. They say, for instance, that black is opposed to white, which at first appears self-evident, but for them there is an element of balance in this contrasting of opposites, and their sense of oneness or completeness is best expressed by contrasting a pair of opposites. Thus the whole tribe consists of the red chiefs and the black commoners—red and black being contrasted as are chiefs and commoners—but together they comprise a balanced entity. A similar mode of expression is found throughout Murle life: thus the dry part of the year, *lomoot* and *tagith*, is contrasted with the wet, *lolongum* and *loola*; and in the kinship context the *abunya* and *kanowanya* are contrasted with the *korgenya* and *toturnya*.[1] It matters not whether a group of half-brothers or a man's wives are being considered—the whole group or homestead is best expressed in Murle thought in this balancing of opposites. In legal

[1] Senior, intermediate, and junior wives, cf. p. 101.

cases the verdict is still announced to the Kelenya and Tangajon
on the east and south, and then to the Ngarotti and Ngenvac on
the west and north. The whole tribe is thought of as four segments
of a circle opposed to the rest of the hostile world.[1] Similarly with
the homestead, the microcosm of the tribe, ideally—if not in practice—it should consist of a man and his four wives with their
families. The exclusiveness or uniqueness of one particular homestead is emphasized by the closing of its rough circle of thorn
hedging against all other homesteads, and yet it is linked by kinship ties with several other homesteads. In the myth of the creation
the maleness of the spirit is contrasted with the femaleness of the
mother's flesh, yet from their union sprang the whole tribe.

The concept of balance is widely used in Murle thought concerning everyday life, but I believe it also pervades their conception of the mystical plane, in that God abides in heaven while
man lives on earth, while the two are linked by the rainbow, the
rain serpent, and the python: of these the Murle say 'They are
one', not in the sense that they are identical, but that they are
co-related. The rainbow is the source of the chief's sacred fire,
the rain serpent is the source of the witch doctor's *kwolo*,[2] and the
python, if met, presages disaster: individually they are all supernatural, and yet together they form a link between the supernatural
in the sky above and the natural on earth below.

Numbers, too, have a great significance. A mother stays in
seclusion four days after the birth of a girl, and three days for a boy:
'four' is considered female and 'three' male. Hence the significance
of the seven stars of the Great Bear and the Little Bear, and still
more of the Pleiades—the unmarried daughters of a Murle chief.
Their religious thought is full of these links between the natural
and the supernatural. In the marriage ceremonies the girl is given
part of the family's sacred firesticks, she carries a spear, the two
families sit on mother earth, she is given a gourd, and those present
are sprinkled with holy water.[3]

14. *Categories of Kinship*

There is a symbolical connection between all the categories of
kinship and the elements of fire and spear, on the one hand, and
earth and water, on the other. In the same way, the four categories
of kinship are related to the four quarters of the earth, in the sense

[1] Cf. p. 47.   [2] Cf. p. 137.   [3] Cf. Chapter VI.

that under the theory of *venon* they correspond with the four points of the compass. Life comes from Jen in the east and death takes the path of the spirits to the west. The universe consists of the sky, with all its supernatural manifestations of God, the earth, on which men spend their lives, and the pit under the earth, whither the spirits repair after death, all being linked in a balanced whole. God is thought of primarily as incomprehensible and inscrutable, organizing the succession of seasons and controlling the rains and floods, the wet years and the dry; omnipresent, yet abiding in the sky; more concerned with his task of controlling the celestial body than with individuals on earth, unless provoked by man's transgression against the laws of nature, when his wrath will surely be manifest to the offending community.

As a result, natural disasters are accepted fatalistically, whereas individual sickness misfortunes are often thought to be due to human machinations, such as witchcraft, cursing, and the evil eye. It is for this reason that they turn to Ngarrec for help, not only in alleviating physical sickness, but in discovering and eradicating the source of spiritual malevolence underlying the physical sickness or misfortune. It was only at the rain dances and the warriors' dances of the drum that prayers or thanksgivings were offered to God by the whole tribe or drumship.[1] The failure of the rains—a comparatively rare occurrence—was felt to be abnormal, an upset in God's ordered plans for the progress of the seasons because something was radically wrong with the world. The transvestism of the ceremonies can be understood in this light, and in the symbolism of Murle thought. The fertilization of women by men was connected in their eyes with the fertilization of the earth by rain, so that in the rain dances Murle women took abnormal action by picking up pieces of dry mud—symbolizing the dry earth—and throwing them at the men of their choice as an invitation—unthinkable at any other time—to sexual intercourse. The euphemism that 'They were praying to God for rain' was resorted to in order to meet an abnormal situation. They were apt to laugh self-consciously when discussing this subject with me, for although it related to their forebears, it was something they had not experienced themselves.

[1] Cf. Chapter IV, pp. 69 et seq.

VIII

THE POLITICAL SYSTEM IN
TRANSITION

THE time-span of this book is roughly that of the Condominium Government, of which I was a servant, from *Mainlorien*, a few years before Lord Kitchener's reconquest of the
Sudan, until the coming of Independence in 1954. With that event
a new chapter opened in Murle history, involving certain inevitable
changes of policy.

Murle history really only begins with their conquest of the Lotilla
country from the Dinka, when the chiefs divided the territory
between the drumships; and the boundaries then agreed upon
stand to this day. Previously events were commemorated in songs
and legends which have been handed down the succeeding generations, but there is insufficient historical data to furnish a study of
their political system covering a period of several generations:
essentially military, it bound the tribe into a closely knit unit for
self-defence, and paradoxically their society was at once extremely
authoritarian and highly democratic. The tribe is now part of a
larger community in mutual toleration with its neighbours; the
tension of constant vigilance against attack has been largely—
although not entirely—relaxed, and as a result their political
system has been put into a state of transition.

When I arrived in Murleland, thirty years after their defeat in
1912 by Government forces, I found their society functioning
much as they said it always had done in the past. The chiefs were
running tribal affairs, for Captain Alban, in his wisdom, had left
the chiefs and elders to try cases in the 'Native courts' he had
instituted. The only apparent significant change was that plaintiffs
could now come to the District Commissioner to register their
complaints, which were referred by him to the chiefs' courts; this
corrected a weakness admitted by the Murle themselves.[1] Initiation
excepted, I found the age-set system and the kinship system, as
far as I could discover, still operating as they had done in the past.

[1] Cf. p. 75.

In the first chapter of this account I stated my conviction that the Murle political system was the result of the interaction of the chiefly, the kinship, and the age-set systems, and I see no reason to quarrel with this hypothesis. It is their interaction within the framework of the fourfold drumship organization which constitutes their political system, and I have used the phrase 'in transition' here because the Murle themselves are so insistent that their way of life is changing—deteriorating would be a more apt description. The older generation clearly think that matters are going from bad to worse, and they advance certain arguments in support of this view which require careful scrutiny, not only to discount the universal predilection of old men to see the time of their youth through rose-tinted spectacles.

The Murle put forward three main arguments in support of their view that the tribe is suffering a decline: *Mainlorien*,[1] the defeat of the Beir Patrol of 1912, and the infertility of their women. In addition they complained to me, as their District Commissioner, that their military organization was in decay, that tribal discipline had suffered and morale deteriorated, and that sickness was rife throughout the tribe. Besides making the prohibition against fighting, they said, the Government had forbidden formal execution by the tribe; thus they laid at the feet of the Government the blame for reducing the effect of the traditional tribal sanctions against adultery and the consequent spread of venereal infections. It was a formidable list—for which the Sudan Government was their scapegoat—and there is evidence to be considered on each count. Bearing in mind Colonel Logan's view that there had been little change in their morals over the years,[2] I viewed these complaints with some reserve. On the other hand, from my own observations they certainly lacked the vitality of the Nuer, with whom I had constant dealings at the time, and there appeared to be fewer Murle children in the villages than amongst their Nuer and Anuak neighbours, although I had no reliable population figures to support my impressions.

[1] Cf. pp. 85, 156.

[2] '. . . If a woman is lazy her husband beats her. If she commits adultery he may overlook the first or second offence, but after that, if she commits herself again, he returns her to her father and demands repayment of the dowry; in the event of there being any children of the marriage, the husband keeps them and forfeits a certain number of the cattle originally paid. Adultery is stated to be fairly common' (Colonel H. Logan, 'Manners and Customs of the Beirs', *Monthly Intelligence Reports*, 1913; *Sudan Notes and Records*, 1918).

As an anthropologist it was fascinating to investigate a tribe so little influenced by the outside world, but as an administrator it was disturbing to find such a feeling of *malaise* abroad in the tribe. The imposition, in isolation, of the sixth commandment on a martial tribe created a vacuum which they could neither understand nor justify.

Their major complaint concerning sickness in general amongst the tribe, and the infertility of their womenfolk in particular, ascribed to the introduction of gonorrhoea by the soldiers of the military garrisons, has, I consider, some validity. Although the young men at the dances still possessed the fine physique noted in early military reports, many of the older men and women were sickly-looking; the Sudan Medical Service did what it could with the facilities available, but they were inadequate. A medical Inspector visited Pibor Post once a year in the Lady Baker Hospital Ship, if the state of the river allowed (frequently there was insufficient water, or the channel was choked with grass and weeds). On these visits large parties of sick people were taken to Malakal Hospital for treatment, but for the rest of the year medical treatment was left to the assistant in charge of the dispensary at Pibor Post, and he frequently ran out of drugs and dressings, owing to the difficulties of communicating with his headquarters at Malakal. Many of the older men suffered from hydrocele, caused by the presence of a parasite in the water they drank. This was noticed as long ago as 1904 by Captain Comyn.[1] Another factor, not, I believe, fully appreciated by the Murle themselves, is the debilitating effect of malaria. Unlike the Nuer and Dinka, who claim to have been created in the plain and to be to some extent inured to malaria, having lived with it for generations, the Murle were originally a mountain people, and I am inclined to think that their descent into the plains is an important factor which has been largely overlooked.

How far the spread of venereal disease was due to the troops I find it impossible to judge, but I consider their admission that the disease was not unknown before the arrival of Government forces should not be ignored. Mentally they appeared to be extremely sane and well-balanced—far more so than their volatile Nilotic neighbours.

The morals of the tribe were fully discussed in Chapter VI, and

[1] *Monthly Intelligence Report,* 1 September 1904.

on balance it appears that, although some deterioration may have occurred during the period under review, it was less than they tried to make me believe, a fact which was substantiated by the early reports. The kinship system, however, although subjected to various stresses and strains by *Mainlorien* and the imposition of an alien rule after 1912, was not in any way radically altered, as the chiefly and age-set systems undoubtedly were, by these two events.

Whatever the real explanation of the monster *mainlorien*, there can be no doubt that some calamity overtook their cattle in the event named after it, *Mainlorien*, about the year 1890;[1] this is borne out by the gradual growth in the number of marriage cattle which has been evident during the last sixty years or so. For a people to whom cattle were and are almost the most important thing in life it must have been a major economic disaster, yet they have recovered, and during the fifties were richer in terms of cattle than most of their Nilotic neighbours. *Mainlorien* by itself, therefore, cannot be regarded as a reason for any basic change in their society.

So far as the Beir Patrol is concerned, they are on safer ground. Here the chiefly system suffered a mortal blow. Previously the chiefs were the intermediaries of the tribe with Heaven, their temporal powers—limited by custom—derived from the supernatural powers they were believed to hold from their position as guardians of the drums. The burning of the senior Tangajon drum, together with the loss of the son and grandson of the Ngarroti chief, were for them an unparalleled military disaster. From that time onwards the chiefs had to submit, to some extent, to the orders of the local representative of the Sudan Government, and the fact that from 1912 to 1924, when the military gave place to the civil administration, the tribe was left very much to its own devices—apart from the prohibitions on raiding their neighbours, execution and ivory poaching—made little real difference to the psychological results of this defeat, because it was the powers of the drums in war that were pre-eminent.

As late as 1936 Mr. Elliot Smith, in his handing-over notes, could write: 'The Murle have never brought a case to the Government', so that the chiefs and elders clearly continued to exercise their judicial powers, although these no longer brought an income

[1] Cf. pp. 85, 154.

to the chiefs, whereas, in the past, to judge from their own accounts, the division of cattle after a successful warlike operation brought considerable rewards for the chief concerned. Thus one of the main pillars of their political system suffered an immeasurable blow to its prestige, and the drum chiefs themselves suffered an actual, if variable, loss of income in terms of cattle.

The Murle also assert that the age-set system suffered as a result of their conquest in 1912, because the initiation—in abeyance since *Mainlorien*—was finally abandoned after this defeat; and it is not wholly unreasonable to accept their own view that it was the cumulative effect of *Mainlorien* and the Beir Patrol some twenty years later. They contend that the chiefs felt there was little point in initiating warriors, since war was denied to them, particularly against their ultimate conquerors armed with modern firearms, to which their spearmen had no effective answer. Inevitably the military organization became slack, for no British-led administration could have tolerated a system whereby every few years a new set of young warriors deliberately sought an opportunity of blooding their spears in battle against their neighbours. There were no captains of age-sets to train and discipline the young men, and very few Murle still possessed shields, let alone carried or made them, yet in the past their use had impressed the officers commanding the Beir Patrols, and the Nuer, too, confirmed to me that when they used them the Murle had been formidable adversaries. There is, therefore, some justification for the chief's insistence that without captains of age-sets they could no longer control the warriors; their own prestige was diminished by the loss of authority and wealth—as they were quick to point out—and during my tenure of office many of them were comparatively poor men in a tribe where wealth, expressed in terms of cattle, was of some significance. For a society so geared to war, the imposition of the *Pax Britannica* required a fundamental readjustment, and this had not taken place; the old system had merely fallen into disuse and decay, and two of the factors in their political system had been adversely affected by historical events. Authority, which may once have been centralized in one person, had been diffused among four drumchiefs, and even they, in spite of their supernatural powers, were bound by tribal custom to listen to the council of elders, who took some delight in quoting precedents and thus limiting the authority of the chiefs even further. Hence my conclusion that, although the Government may have speeded up the alleged decline in the power of the chiefs, and in tribal discipline—which remained strong in the outward respect accorded to age—a historical tendency in this direction was already evident long before the Government took charge.

Korok Adeng was tacitly accepted to be the senior chief because he represented the senior Tangajon line, although the Ngarroti were inclined to resent this as they were more numerous and far wealthier than the Tangajon. Yet, if the Kelenya claims are to be taken seriously, a few generations ago their drumchief must, on the analogy of the kinship system, have occupied a commanding position, not far short of that of paramount priest-king of the tribe. Such is the respect paid to seniority in family and lineage affairs, that it seems probable that an equal respect must have been accorded to the Kelenya chief, whom everyone admitted had pride of place in the past in tribal affairs. This, however, is speculation, for the Kelenya—and Ngenvac—lost their drum long before the period covered by this account and there is no means of knowing his real position. Although they speak of four drumships the loss of the Kelenya and Ngenvac drums has to be borne in mind; so, too, the fact that the Tangajon and Ngarroti drums had split, and the division of the conquered territory recognized this state of affairs, producing two opposed halves, Kelenya and Tangajon on the one hand and Ngarroti and Ngenvac on the other. The division of the tribe into 'four' drumships corresponds exactly with the four categories of kinship and the four huts of one man in an ideal homestead. In the latter pattern the centre is the place of power and the place of blessing, suggesting that at one time there was a central place of authority. I found no central political authority, only the four drumships, each receiving its segment from the central point of Mount Lothir. A Tangajon marriage song runs: 'I am the right hand with the first spear amongst the warriors'; a Longarim song tells of Keboh with his shield (worn on the left arm), bringing back a drum to his village; the Kelenya song contains the proud boast *'ken abu udana'*, 'I am the head'; while the Ngarroti are spoken of as the *'barkory'*, the back or rump.

Unfortunately, the Sudan Government appeared on the Murle scene as 'friends' of their traditional Dinka enemies, and this may have been the final disillusionment that led them to adopt a policy of passive resistance to their conquerors; the early military reports from Pibor Post contained ample evidence of their reluctance to co-operate, for their labour was unsatisfactory, and they admitted to me that, bribed with presents of meat and rifles, they used to help the Abyssinian ivory poachers against whose inroads the military administration had to devote so much of their time.

Another inevitable difficulty was that the Murle, who spoke the tongues of their Nilotic neighbours readily enough, did not find Arabic easy, and there was always a shortage of reliable interpreters. At this distance in time it is almost impossible to assess the full psychological effects on the tribe, although for them it was fortunate that from 1912 to 1945 the infrequent transfer of their British administrators provided a stability not common in many parts of Africa, where frequent changes of officials have been a stumbling block to progress and mutual understanding. Events have proved, however, that neither the military nor the civil administration gave the Murle sufficient leadership, and this, perhaps, is the greatest failure on the part of the Government. The development of Pibor District was distressingly slow, even by Sudan standards. A remote corner of the most backward province, it counted for little with the central Government, which had other and more pressing problems on its hands. The local administration, both military and civil, did their best with the scant resources available, but their actions were, to a large extent, governed by their instructions from Khartoum, and these in turn were influenced by the economic position of the country as a whole. Thus, after the world economic crisis of 1929–31, when retrenchment was the order of the day, the late Sir Stewart Symes, then Governor-General, put the administration of the Upper Nile Province on to a care-and-maintenance basis. District budgets were cut to a minimum, and it was almost impossible to obtain funds for any kind of development. It was not until after the Second World War that there were sufficient funds to set up a development budget, when the Jonglei Investigation Team, after completing their report on the proposed canal, were converted into a Southern Development Investigation Team in 1953. Prior to this the Southern Provinces were administered according to the so-called Southern Policy—an amalgam of economic necessity and altruistic ideals—which held sway from the murder of Sir Lee Stack in 1924 until the last few years of Sir James Robertson's tenure of the Civil Secretaryship (1952–4). This recognized that the peoples of the

south were Africans and regarded as slaves by all but a few edu-
cated Northern Sudanese. Practically all education, and most
medical work, were left to Christian missions. Economically
this was the cheapest approach, but politically it had the dis-
advantage of tending to accentuate rather than minimize the differences between the two parts of the Sudan, and it undoubtedly
delayed development of the Southern Provinces. It is not for me
to criticize this policy here, nor am I concerned with the rights
and wrongs of the matter, but rather with the effects of colonial
rule (almost the lack of it) on the tribe in question.

From 1936 onwards chiefs' courts were established and the
District Commissioner of the day tried to ensure that they func-
tioned for the settlement of cases; tribute, at first paid in bulls
and later in money, was levied; primitive roads and some useful
bridges were made; shops slowly increased in number; and
Government medical and veterinary services were gradually augmented. As a result, money began to supplement the cattle-and-
sheep economy, and the Murle started to buy more and more of
their hoes, spears, beds, cloth, and tobacco from Northern
Sudanese merchants instead of bartering with their neighbours.
Eventually an American Mission was opened at Pibor Post, followed by a school now taken over by the Education Department,
so that Christianity and Islam have been introduced to the tribe,
and a number of children have learned English or Arabic. It will
be interesting to see if the new-found fertility in Murle women
will curb the illicit trade in 'incest children', for cattle, with the
Bor Dinka, a practice frowned upon by authority, but difficult to
prevent.

The most persistent outside influences on the tribe since Independence in 1955 will probably prove to have been Arabic and
Islamic. The geographical position of the district, however, makes
it likely that they will go on living much as they always have done,
for their way of life is governed by the natural conditions, and it
seems that their customs will not be greatly changed by outside
events for a number of years. On the other hand, they will inevitably have more and more dealings with their neighbours on a
peaceful, as opposed to the former warlike, basis, and this should
modify the exclusiveness of the Murle as the years progress.

I wish them well.

APPENDICES

A. CATTLE-HORN CONFORMATIONS

One horn up and one down	*Ngelec*
Pointing straight down	*Moot*
Normal semi-circular horns	*Uwalan*
Tips tied together when young; they form a circle but later the tips turn forwards	*Nyakodhoth*
Hornless	*Karro*
Very short horns pointing straight upwards	$\begin{cases} Adoiyo \\ Adoiyotho \end{cases}$
Up and out to start with, but later with tips turned forwards	*Dokom*

The basic cattle colours, bayen, *are*:

Red	*Ci meri*
Black	*Ci oli*
Bay (lit. 'green')	*Ci colai*
White	*Ci vor*
With small white spots	*Ci budhen*
Striped or patched in black and white (cf. zebra)	*Ci labac*
With red spots (cf. giraffe)	*Ci aric* or *Karri*
Yellow	*Ci man*
Grey	*Ci gidang*
Red, with white patches on face and flanks	*Ci dhurial*
White-faced	*Ci bulka*
White on belly and white back	*Ci nguro*
Black back with white flanks (as an ostrich)	*Ci labok*
Black without any white markings (as a bull buffalo)	*Ci dhuri*
Brindled (as a crocodile)	*Ci tulkec*

B. CATTLE TERMS

The general term for cattle is *tang*, pl. *ten*, *ronginit* being used for a herd of cattle.

They are divided by age and sex as follows:

Bull	*Ole*
Ox	*Arith*
Large Ox	*Koromae* *Tomot* *Motododo*
Young Ox	*Bobonglori*
Heifer	*Buthongit*
Calf	*Mol*

Cows are referred to as:

Old cow	*Gaalac*
Old barren cow	*Nyakaluk*
Young barren cow	*Abudan*
Good milker	*Tang c'adotanne*
Bad milker	*Durec*
Cow in milk	*Tang c'anoiyi*
Cow with only enough milk to feed its calf	*Anyuvnayav*
Dry cow	*Tang c'uweth*
Cow and calf	*Golec*
Cow with its first calf	*Tang ci ngantiyan*

INDEX